All About African Violets

by MONTAGUE FREE

Revised and Expanded by
CHARLES MARDEN FITCH

HERE, in a newly revised and expanded edition, is Montague Free's classic work on how to successfully propagate and care for African-violets. Updated by Charles Marden Fitch, internationally respected horticulturist and photographer, this book provides extensive information on all aspects of growing this popular house plant.

All the helpful ingredients of the original edition are here, with the addition of new sections on pesticides, light gardening, soil-free mixes, plant patents, modern hybrids, and purchasing plants and supplies.

Among the book's 125 color and black-and-white photographs are examples of the most popular and newest varieties of saintpaulias, as well as sequence pictures which give step-by-step directions on propagating, potting, watering, and fertilizing your plants.

Written in a lively, entertaining, non-technical style, this excellent reference book supplies all that's new and contemporary in producing healthy, hand-

(continued on back flap)

York.

ALL ABOUT AFRICAN VIOLETS

All About
AFRICAN
ఌ VIOLETS ఌ

The Complete Guide
to Success
with Saintpaulias

By MONTAGUE FREE
Revised and Expanded by
CHARLES MARDEN FITCH

DOUBLEDAY & COMPANY, INC.

GARDEN CITY, N.Y.

Library of Congress Cataloging in Publication Data

Free, Montague, 1885–1965.
    All about African violets.

    Includes index.
    1. African violets. I. Fitch, Charles Marden.
II. Title.
SB413.A4F7 1979   635.9′33′81

27330

Contents

List of Illustrations

COLOR PHOTOGRAPHS
By Charles Marden Fitch

HALFTONES

CREDITS, Halftone Photographs

Charles Marden Fitch: 32, 33, 34, 43, 44, 45, 47, 51, 55, 63, 68, 72, 74, 75, 85, 142, 152, 157, 162, 169, 173, 190, 228, 231.

Steenson and Baker: 23, 24, 26, 27, 28, 31, 38, 52, 76, 77, 78, 79, 80, 91, 92, 94, 99, 100, 102, 106, 107, 109, 110, 112, 113, 117, 118, 145, 148, 150, 160, 184, 185, 187, 188, 191, 192, 193, 194, 195, 196, 197, 198, 199, 200, 201, 202, 210, 211, 212, 213, 217, 219, 220, 222, 225, 226, 227.

Malby and Company: 18

U. S. Dept of Agriculture: 98

J. A. Nearing Company, Inc.: 166

Foreword to Revised Edition

Author Montague Free was a horticulturist at the Brooklyn Botanic Garden for thirty-one years. He grew a wide variety of exotic plants and especially appreciated the African-violets. His book *All About African Violets* has been a favorite reference for many years. Montague Free's writing is based on his personal experience with growing saintpaulias. His pleasure with African-violets, and personal contact with other African-violet growers, shows in these pages. Since Mr. Free wrote his original book, the African-violet breeders have introduced several new types of hybrids and hundreds of registered clones. Although new, these modern plants respond to the same cultural advice presented by Mr. Free. The author's book remains valuable because it is based on his personal experience.

Nelson Doubleday Books invited me to supplement Mr. Free's original *All About African Violets* with current information in several areas. Therefore in this revised edition you will find my recommendations for selecting modern hybrids, a new chapter about sources for plants and supplies, new information about pesticides, light gardening, and many new photographs. Montague Free's enthusiasm and firsthand accounts remain and make this book a valuable addition in any gardener's library.

Charles Marden Fitch

Praise and Thanksgiving
(Foreword to the Original Edition)

To my wife, for never fussing (well, hardly ever!) about the disruption of our home by an influx of more than a hundred saintpaulias and by the traipsing in and out of photographers who, it seemed, always came on cleaning days. Her complaints of water drips on the furniture and chicken grits and soil on the floor were mild indeed. Actually she was bitten by the saintpaulia bug herself and on more than one occasion "wiped my eye" by growing better plants with bigger flowers than mine. I supplied the soil and did the potting, though!

To the late Kenneth Steenson (of Steenson and Baker, Poughkeepsie, New York) who was responsible for many of the photographs that illustrate this book. He spared no pains to arrive at first-class results and, in the process, became a saintpaulia fan.

To Freeman A. Weiss, formerly Senior Pathologist of the Bureau of Plant Industry, U.S.D.A., for "vetting" the material on growing conditions and avoiding saintpaulia troubles.

To Edward Wentink of Rose Acre Nurseries, Salisbury Mills, New York, for putting the facilities of his establishment at my disposal. He did not seem to mind in the least when we interfered with the orderly running of his greenhouses in the process of making pictures of choice varieties.

To Neil C. and Mary J. Miller, for their investigation of home treatments against mites and nematodes; and for many hints obtained from them in conversation.

To the African Violet Society of America, for information gleaned from the pages of the *African Violet Magazine,* and to two past presidents—Alma Wright and Myrtle Radtke—in particular, who were most courteous and helpful in obtaining and providing some needed pictures, and in many other ways.

MONTAGUE FREE

ALL ABOUT AFRICAN VIOLETS

Ramonda pyrenaica, *a close relative of the African-violet, has purple or white flowers and survives zero temperatures outdoors with protection.*

CHAPTER 1

What are African Violets?

Let us make it clear from the start that African-violets (saintpaulia) are not true Violets (Violas). They belong in the plant family *Gesneriaceae,* the most familiar members of which, apart from African-violets, are Gloxinia and Cupid's Bower or Magic Flower (Achimenes). The member of this family most closely approaching African-violets in general appearance is Ramonda, a genus of about ten species native to the mountains of Europe.

Saintpaulia was discovered by the imperial district governor of Usambara in East Africa who sent seeds (or plants) to his father Baron Walter von St. Paul-Illaire in Germany about 1890. St. Paul-Illaire brought the plants to the attention of the botanist Herman Wendland, director of the Royal Botanie Gardens at Herrenhausen, who described the species and gave it the name *Saintpaulia ionantha.* (Actually, there were two species in the original shipment as discussed in Chapter 12.) The genus name *Saintpaulia,* of course, commemorates the family of the discoverer and introducer; the specific name ionantha comes from the Greek, meaning "with flowers like a Violet." Apparently Wendland was responsible for the use of the word "Violet" in the common name (*Das Violette Usambara*), which is rather surprising coming from a botanist. In English the common names are: Usambara Violet, East African Violet, and African-violet; with the latter in most common usage.

While I think the name saintpaulia should be preferred because it is correct, euphonious, easy to pronounce and spell, I have no unsurpassable objection to African-violet as a name provided the distinguishing adjective "African" is retained—both names are used interchangeably in this book. But lately many people have fallen into the habit of calling saintpaulias just "Violets," which is misleading. This has already resulted in wasted efforts on the part of those who, unfamiliar with the fact that their botanical relationship is remote enough to inhibit a successful "take," have tried to produce the elusive yellow saintpaulia by crossing African-violets with one or more of the native yellow true Violets which belong in the genus *Viola*.

Representatives of the genus *Saintpaulia* are found in varied habitats in Tanzania, formerly Tanganyika Territory, the altitude in which they grow ranging from 30 to 150 feet above sea level in the Tanga area (*S. ionantha*), to around 3,000 feet in the East Usambara Mountains (*S. diplotricha*) and near the summit of Mt. Tongwe (*S. tongwensis*). They are usually rooted in humus in crevices of limestone and gneiss rocks, but always in some shade, heavy or light.

EARLY DEVELOPMENT

My first acquaintance with African-violets was about fifty years ago when I saw them growing under the name *Saintpaulia ionantha* in the tropical greenhouses of the University Botanic Garden of Cambridge, England, where I was employed as a gardener. At that time saintpaulias had only recently been introduced to cultivation from German East Africa (now Tanzania) and they were seldom seen except in botanic gardens and the plant houses of large estates. No one, I suppose, and certainly not I, had any idea of the popularity they were to achieve as the most widely grown house plants in the United States. In those early days saintpaulia was thought to be rather delicate in constitution, needing a humid, tropical atmosphere provided by a greenhouse. Now we know it is one of the toughest and most adaptable of plants for house culture.

Although saintpaulias were widely grown by European gardeners and some few varieties were segregated, such as *albescens, grandiflora, purpurea,* and *variegata,* it was not until about 1926, when Armacost and Royston, a California firm, introduced a number of named varieties, that they began to come into their own. These varieties were selections from the plants raised from seeds received from Europe as *Saintpaulia ionantha.* Among them were such well-known varieties as 'Admiral', 'Amethyst', 'Blue Boy' (the pre-eminent commercial variety), 'Commodore', and 'Neptune', all good varieties, still grown by some connoisseurs, although pushed out of commercial catalogues by recent introductions. Armacost and Royston no longer raise saintpaulias, but the excellence of those they released to the trade and the impetus given to commercial culture by their introduction are largely responsible for the popularity of African-violets today.

As soon as it was discovered that saintpaulias would thrive in an ordinary dwelling, even under the care of the veriest tyro, the interest in them increased to an amazing extent so that it is now easily the most popular house plant, being grown for sale by the hundred thousand by commercial florists and to a lesser extent by "semipros." Thousands of distinct varieties are now available to tease the palate of the collector, and the end is nowhere in sight. But enough of species and varieties for now—they will be discussed more fully in Chapter 12.

VARIETIES

It is not necessary to scurry around and invent reasons for saintpaulias' phenomenal rise in favor. The charm of their flowers and, in the case of some of the modern varieties, the beauty and distinction of their foliage are enough to endear them. There is a wide color range in the flowers, from white through pale "blue" to deep purple, and from pink to almost red. The flower size varies according to variety, culture, age of plant, and season—from the ½-inch flowers of miniatures to 3-inch flowers on standard hybrids such as 'Winter's Dream' and 'Wild Country'. There is just as much variety in their leaf characters: some are long and narrow, as in the curiously named 'Blue Longifolia Crenulate'; others are almost orbicular, as in the Du Pont series. Some are flat; others have their edges turned up so that they are said to be "spooned"; still other varieties, just to be contrary, turn their leaf margins downward; and occasionally both types may be found on one plant. In many of the varieties the veins are much depressed, giving the leaf a quilted appearance, and in some ('Old Lace' is an example) this is so pronounced that the leaf is pleasantly blistered; and in some hybrids the leaves are fluted. The leaf margins, especially on the young leaves, are toothed, but the teeth may disappear with age even as they do in humans; sometimes they are deeply scalloped, or even lobed, and in some varieties they are waved or ruffled. In color they may be pale green, deep green, or bronzed on the upper surface; and the underside may be silvery white, flushed with rose, or cabbage red. In the Girl series the leaves of certain varieties remind one of those of a Zonal Geranium, with a colored blotch at the junction of blade and petiole which may be creamy white, pinkish, or bronze.

One could slightly paraphrase Shakespeare and say: "age doth not wither them nor custom stale their infinite variety." This applies not only to the group as a whole but also to individual plants whose mutability in the case of some varieties seems to be almost unlimited. A plant just beginning to bloom may present an entirely different aspect as it ages. Often it starts off with flowers held erect in the center of the crown; as the days pass, new leaves develop, the flowers continue to unfold on the original peduncles so that finally they are held almost horizontally, forming an informal ring of flowers between two tiers of leaves, giving the effect of a colonial bouquet.

Fantastic Changeability   This is one of the most fascinating characteristics of saintpaulias, especially in the case of the newer varieties, whose inheritance may be mixed and their chromosome number altered. Sometimes the upsetting factor can be attributed to environment, sometimes to an inherent tendency to variation, and sometimes to mutation (sporting).

For example, two plants of 'Tinted Lady' were purchased from two sources at about the same time. Anyone not familiar with saintpaulias would say, "Here are two distinct varieties," but both agree on the characteristics which distinguish 'Tinted Lady'—the shape of the pale flowers; the venation, texture, and shape of the leaves are the same; where they differ is in their general appearance caused by environment. One plant, obtained from a commercial amateur who had no greenhouse, has abnormally long leafstalks because of crowding and insufficient light; the other is a normal, compact, well-shaped plant brought about by adequate spacing and ample illumination provided by a greenhouse.

Different growing conditions may affect appearance of plants of the same variety. 'Tinted Lady' plant at right is lanky, probably from overcrowding and poor light, while 'Tinted Lady' at left, grown in a greenhouse, is shapely and compact.

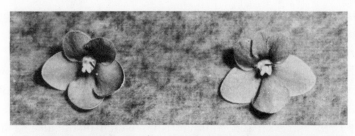

Flowers of the same variety may differ. Top left: normal 'Viking' flower; right: extra petal. Below left: normal 'Du Pont No. 1'; right: with abnormal petal, forming the star-type flower.

The Du Pont series of varieties produces large flowers which often depart from the normal. In the accompanying illustration, the lowermost flower at the left represents the usual pattern of Du Pont 'Blue No. 1'—a pair of comparatively small petals at the top, two broad-spreading "wings," and a large lower lip. All the petals of its neighbor from the same plant, on the other hand, are almost the same size and shape, making the corolla nearly regular; and it has double its quota of stamens. This increase in the number of stamens also commonly occurs on my plant of 'Du Pont Lavender Pink', but in this case the phenomenon usually is accompanied by a reduction of the number of petals to four.

The flowers in the top row of the same photograph are from the variety 'Viking'—one has the typical characteristics of saintpaulias in general; the other has one extra petal. On looking later at the plant these flowers came from, I found it carrying a flower with *two* extra petals, which might indicate a tendency toward "doubling" were it not for the fact that occasionally the plant bears flowers with only four petals!

Other Inconsistencies An aberrancy sometimes seen in certain varieties, notably 'Dainty Maid' and 'White Lady', is a tendency toward topsy-turviness—some of the flowers, instead of carrying the two smaller petals uppermost, get themselves twisted around so that they are upside down or sideways.

Inconstancies of this nature, occurring as they do on the same plant, cannot be ascribed to environment, but rather to inherited tendencies.

Many of the most striking variations which affect saintpaulias are the result of bud mutations (sports) arising from leaf cuttings. My first intimation of the tendency of saintpaulias to mutate came several years ago when a reader of *The Home Garden* magazine wrote to the "Question Box" saying that she had rooted a leaf of a pink variety which gave rise to seven plantlets—one of which produced pink flowers, one white, and five dark blue.

The Amazon and Supreme varieties, such as 'Amazon Pink Beauty', 'Orchid Beauty Amazon', and 'Blue Boy Supreme', characterized by heavier, more rounded leaves and larger flowers (but less freely produced), originated as bud sports of the varieties whose name they bear.

The most startling variations I have ever seen of this nature occurred in a plant of the variety 'Helen Wilson'. This is a seedling variety with double purple flowers and Girl-type foliage originated by Frank Tinari. During a visit to Tinari Greenhouses I saw hundreds, perhaps thousands, of young plants, raised from leaf cuttings of this seedling, which exhibited an amazing variety of leaf shape and pattern. I picked out two of the extremes and brought them home to be photographed. One plant is practically normal, but the leaves of the other are so lobed and divided that they look like compound leaves. One of them, not visible in the

Two 'Helen Wilson' plants show variations. Normal plant at left; lobed-leaved at right. Two months later the lobed plant resumed normal growth and soon resembled its neighbor.

photograph, has a large lobe depending from the underside of the midrib. It should be recorded that a month or so after the picture was made, the plant started to produce normal leaves, thus giving further evidence of its fickleness.

Just what causes these violent changes from the normal it is difficult to say with any assurance. Probably it is a matter of mixed-up genes (inheritance factors) owing to crossing, and to the fact that the plants are subjected to an environment and methods of propagation very different from those experienced by saintpaulias in nature.

Another saintpaulia quirk was exemplified when a neighbor put in two leaf cuttings, one of which, instead of producing the usual crop of plantlets, sent up a solitary flower which in itself is a freak, having an extra petal and no stamens whatever. At the time of writing, this leaf has developed another blossom and there are indications that it is about to give birth to a plantlet.

New plantlets may be produced in the queerest places. Ordinarily they originate from the base of the stalk when a leaf is inserted as a cutting, but there are instances recorded where they show up at intervals all along the stalk; or even on the veins, both upper and lower, of the leaf blade. Occasionally one may see plantlets developing on the flower stalks.

Spooning Some varieties in which the edges of the leaves turn upward are said to be "spooned"—'Neptune', 'Blue Eyes', et cetera. The spooning nature of saintpaulia seems to be unstable. I have two plants of 'Neptune' bought at about the same time; one is now showing signs of spooning, but leaves of the other, which came as "Spoon Neptune," are as flat as pancakes. One might surmise that spooning in saintpaulias is, as it is with humans, a mature or adolescent phenomenon, but I had some seedlings which were distinctly spooned and scooped (almost-

Instead of producing leaves, a saintpaulia leaf cutting has sent up one solitary flower which has an extra petal and no stamens.

funnel-shaped) when they were mere babies and lost the character before they were a year old! There is no telling where you are with saintpaulias. It is well known that leaf cuttings sometimes will wait a year or longer before propagating, while others root and start making plantlets within a few weeks. These differences I have always attributed either to varietal idiosyncrasies or to the time of insertion.

Neither of these factors applies in the case of leaves from a plant of 'Redhead Supreme', which were accidentally broken from a plant early in February. The stalks were cut to regulation length (1½ inches) and inserted side by side in a propagating case so there was absolutely no difference in environment. And yet four months later one had rooted vigorously and produced a good crop of plantlets, while the other had barely rooted with no signs of propagation, as shown in the accompanying photograph. The only suggestion I can make to account for the difference is that one leaf was a little more mature than its neighbor. But this explanation is not universally applicable because at about the same time I put in eight leaves (of another variety), ranging from very young to middle-aged, with no difference in

Leaf cutting of 'Redhead Supreme' (left) formed sparse roots, while its companion (right) made a good crop of roots and several plantlets and is well on the way toward flowering.

the number of plantlets produced that could be attributed to degree of maturity. It's all very puzzling and one can only assume that here two factors are involved—degree of maturity, plus the nature of the variety.

Saintpaulias ordinarily can be expected to progress, not in a humdrum and prosaic way, for they are always glamorous, but in a manner that is orderly and predictable. Then, suddenly, one or more plants, sometimes without apparent reason, will go haywire, throw their hats over the windmill, and develop strange new habits—which just adds to the fascination of growing them.

Adaptability Beauty of plant and interesting behavior are not the main causes for their tremendous popularity, which chiefly can be attributed to their floriferousness and adaptability to home culture. It is not unusual for them to bloom without cessation for a year or more, and their finest display comes during the winter months, when flowers are most appreciated. By taking proper precautions as to shading and protection from cold they will thrive in any aspect, producing their flowers freely even when kept in north-facing windows. They also may be grown in a cellar with no light at all except that supplied by electricity. The only thing that seems to really inhibit blossoming is impure air—especially when it is contaminated with artificial cooking gas. One of their appealing traits is that they start to bloom in infancy (four to nine months) and continue, either constantly or at intervals, for many years.

Because there are thousands of varieties, they are exceptionally good collectors' items; more especially as they are small enough, or can be so maintained by cultural modifications, to permit a large number to be contained in a comparatively small space. On the other hand, if the minutiae which appeal to the collector have no place in your scheme of things and you prefer a few extra-large plants rather than many small ones, you can, if you are a skillful cultivator and select the right varieties (see Chapter 8), grow plants from 2 to 2½ feet across. A greenhouse is not needed to grow these enormous plants—as a matter of fact, I believe the largest plants ever exhibited were grown in parlor, bedroom, or bath. One seldom sees very large plants in the greenhouse of commercial growers, perhaps because they are unable to supply the demand for flowering plants which are avidly snapped up by customers before they reach the large specimen stage.

Another asset possessed by saintpaulias is the small size of their root system. Large pots are neither necessary nor desirable in which to grow them. Plants will flower in 2¼-inch pots, and good specimens can be grown in the 3½-inch size, which is a big advantage when shelf space is limited and the grower is not a husky who takes pleasure in bearing heavy weights. It is seldom desirable to use pots in excess of 4½ inches except in the case of the strong-growing Du Pont and similar varieties, mature plants of which require 5- or 6-inch bulb or seed pans.

There is almost no ledge, table, or mantel contained in a home which cannot accommodate a saintpaulia—for a time, at any rate. Saintpaulias can be grown or displayed on window sills or on shelves attached to the window casing. In well-lighted rooms they can be grown well away from the windows if so desired, on mantels, or coffee tables, and can be used for weeks on end as a centerpiece on the dining table. At least one African-violet devotee has made a set of shelves recessed like the stories of a modern skyscraper, mounted on wheels or casters in the manner of a tea wagon so that the plants can easily be wheeled from place to place or from room to room to take advantage of favorable light and temperature conditions. You can grow saintpaulias under fluorescent lights almost anywhere.

In addition to orthodox methods of growing and displaying them in flowerpots they can be planted in Strawberry jars, terrariums, fish bowls (without their usual concomitants of fish and water), or in indoor window boxes. They may also be associated with other plants in shallow, broad pans, in holes made in porous rocks, or planted in depressions of pieces of picturesque driftwood.

Maidenhair Fern provides a filmy green background for 'Snow White' (center) with plants of 'Pink Beauty' on each side.

SAINTPAULIA COMPANIONS

The flowers of African-violets are always beautiful, and when these are produced in conjunction with distinctive foliage the plants are impressive in their own right and, like good wine, need no bush. But some of the most floriferous varieties do not have especially attractive leaves, and their flowers at certain stages of growth may be untidily displayed on sprawling horizontal stalks. It seemed to me that their appearance could be enhanced if associated with contrasting foliage, so I have tried combining them with other plants in the same container to provide a background and a foil.

So far my most successful companion planting is one pictured here, which has in the foreground *Saintpaulia* 'Snow White' flanked on either side with 'Pink Beauty', and with florists' Maidenhair Fern (*Adiantum cuneatum*) in the background. I was fortunate in being able to get from a local florist a Fern-dish liner 3 inches deep and 9 inches across—just about the right size. With the passing of the Fern dish, which used to be an integral part of the well-furnished dining table in the early part of the century, I understand these liners are scarce articles, so it may be necessary to use a substitute, such as an old-time shallow soup tureen (get someone to drill a hole through the bottom), or a wooden salad bowl spar-varnished to prevent warping.

The Fern I used was growing in a 3-inch pot, which made it necessary to flatten the root ball somewhat in order to bring its surface below the rim of the liner. The saintpaulias were taken from 2½-inch pots and presented no difficulty. Regular African-violet soil was used. This seems to suit the Fern a little too well, if anything, considering its vigorous growth, which now needs

The Rhapsodie hybrids are bred for vigor and a constant flowering habit. In rear are pink 'Claudia' (left) and dark blue 'Elfriede'. In front are 'Claudia' (left) and 'Gisela', a light pink single.

Trailing African-violets are now offered by many dealers. This bushy basket plant growing near a bright window is 'Mysterium', a semidouble pink-flowered hybrid developed by Lyndon Lyon.

Miniature hybrid 'Tiny Pink', bred by Lyndon Lyon, takes up very little space yet produces many flowers. This plant is growing in a 1½-inch plastic pot.

curbing by the removal of some of the larger fronds. The photograph was made a little more than four months after the "arrangement" was planted.

Other combinations tried, though not 100 per cent successful
so far, are: 'White Lady' perched in a soil-filled crevice made
by putting two pieces of porous tufa rock in another liner, with
a Crested Brake Fern for background (it grew too vigorously,
but this can be corrected by pruning), with the tufted *Selaginella
browni* nestling at the base and a Panamiga (*Pilea involucrata*)
nearby, which grows well enough in association but has foliage
too much like that of saintpaulia. Another setup is of *Saintpaulia* 'Viking', Babys-tears (Helxine), a narrow-leaved
Maranta, and *Cryptanthus acaulis,* a terrestrial bromeliad. The
base for this is a platter filched from my wife's china closet and
filled to the rim with soil. On this is set a piece of tufa rock with
a soil-filled cavity in which the saintpaulia is planted. The other
plants are disposed in the soil around the base of the rock. I am
reserving judgment on this, but so far it is my least effective attempt. The African-violet, though healthy, is dwarfed (not
enough soil?); the Babys-tears is spindling (not enough light)
and shows a tendency to overrun everything—which, however,
could be curbed by judicious use of my wife's shears, if she
would agree to lend them and I had time to use them.

For the benefit of those who would like to get into the game,
here are a few suitable background companions: *An-
thurium scherzerianum, Begonia foliosa, Syagrus* (*Cocos*) *wed-
delliana,* and *Cyperus alternifolius nanus.*

Others worth trying are *Davallia pentaphylla* (Fern), *Dra-
caena sanderiana* (will ultimately grow too tall), *Pilea micro-
phylla* (Artillery Plant), and *Tillandsia lindeniana,* a bromeliad.

Companion planting is a fascinating addendum to saintpaulia
culture with lots of possibilities. It calls merely for plants which
will thrive under the same conditions accorded African-violets
but not so vigorously that they crowd them out. A close watch
must be kept to prevent this, either by pruning of top and/or
roots or by removal of the offender if pruning does not suffice.

CHAPTER 2

Growing Conditions

Saintpaulias in their native home in East Africa grow in primeval forest and wooded places which doubtless contributes to their ability to thrive in the often rather dim surroundings accorded them in our homes. Although an east window is believed by many to provide the most desirable aspect for them, it is the amount of light they receive rather than their orientation that is the determining factor. In our home we have them growing in north, east, south, and west aspects, and it would be difficult for me to tell in which window they thrive best.

ASPECT

Undiluted sunshine is not desirable except perhaps during the shortest days of winter in the north, and in very early morning. The bulk of my plants are grown in the study, which has a large bay window facing the south and another window to the west and so is well lighted.

Approximately fifty varieties are accommodated on an especially constructed plant bench in a bay window. During the shortest days of winter no shading is necessary, but from February to mid-May and from the end of September until mid-November they are shaded by plastic curtains which can be drawn back to admit more light whenever it seems desirable. During the summer, when the large Sugar Maples are in full leaf, no shading is necessary except for an hour or two before noon when the sun shines through the gap between two trees.

About twenty plants are accommodated on top of built-in bookshelves, 4 feet high and 12 feet back from the south window. These never get any direct sun but the light is fairly good, especially as the walls are deliberately left white to reflect light rather than to absorb it. There is considerable traffic back and forth between these two locations; plants newly received, especially if their roots were injured in transit, are kept in the comparatively dim light of the shelf until they have recuperated. Young plants large enough to bloom are kept in the well-lighted bay until they produce flower buds and then are transferred to the shelf if their room is needed in the bay.

In the west window an ex-aquarium containing a 3-inch layer of sand and peat moss sits on the radiator. Leaves broken off by accident or otherwise are inserted to form new plants. During summer, when the heat is off, the aquarium is flanked at each end by two wick-watered saintpaulias. No artificial shade is provided here, but from mid-May until fall a large Maple shuts out the westerly sun.

In the kitchen my wife has a large plant of 'Blue Boy' supported in a hanging pot attached to a bracket fastened to the upright between two south-facing windows. During April and early May this gets a little too much sun, and a few flowers were sunburned, but the upright casts enough shade to prevent any real damage and a blessed Sugar Maple takes care of the shade situation during the summer. Incidentally, this plant brought from a north window improved in its new location—whether it enjoyed the additional light or whether the result was owing to increased humidity brought about by water vapor from dishwashing it is impossible to say.

Upstairs in the east window of my bedroom is a yard-long "self-watering" window box pack-jammed with three dozen seed-

African-violets are often injured by cold drafts, the leaves showing a characteristic white blotching.

lings. These are shaded by a thin curtain on the lower half of the sash whenever it seems necessary.

In a west window, with the same shade conditions as downstairs, we have glass shelves and a watertight tray filled with pebbles in which water is kept. The saintpaulias do well both on shelves and tray, but on one below-zero night, when a howling gale was blowing, enough cold air found its way through chinks (in spite of storm sash) to injure plants on the shelves. This is a factor that must be taken into account by growers of saintpaulia in cold climates—plants in north and west windows must be moved away from the window on cold, windy nights or some effective insulation, such as cardboard or newspapers, placed between them and the glass. In warmer climates, a window sill is perfectly safe.

My wife has saintpaulias growing in her sewing room, which has south and west windows shaded by thin curtains, and in an unoccupied room with a north window. She believes she gets better results in the north window.

The foregoing is intended to give an inkling of how the aspect situation is handled in one household. The thin curtains we use in south, east, and west windows might have to be replaced with heavier ones during the summer months were it not for the large Maples just beyond the windows.

Actually it is impossible to lay down any hard-and-fast rule regarding the amount of shading necessary to provide optimum results. Light intensity varies in accordance with geographical location, the season of the year, and the state of the weather. Snow on the ground, by its reflecting quality, affects the quantity of light in the room; so does the color of the walls and furnishings—dark walls absorb light, pale colors reflect it. In general, I would say that if you live in a region where sunshine is abundant, north windows would furnish satisfactory growing conditions provided there is no overhead shade outdoors to cut out sky-shine. The next choice would be an east or west window with thin curtains to dilute the sun during the hottest months; but south windows will be quite all right provided enough shade is given to prevent the foliage from turning yellow and the flowers from scorching.

Let the Plants Guide You   The most important thing I can say with reference to this subject is to let the plants guide you to the right aspect for them. If the leaves are lush and no flowers are produced, more light is needed; if, on the other hand, all the leaves are yellowish and you are sure it is not because of starvation, you can assume that the sun is their undoing. If the plants do not thrive in one aspect and you are sure that soil and watering are not at fault (see Chapters 3 and 4), don't be misled by the old wives' tale that "African-violets should *never* be moved," but try them in different locations until one is found that suits them. In this connection you may find, in common with many others, that a seasonal change is desirable—south, east, or west windows in winter; north windows in summer.

I have seen African-violets grown successfully in an east window, each in its own saucer on a simple stand, looking like an open-front bookcase without any back, its base resting on the floor, with width enough to fill the window space. The shelves, 6 inches wide, started just below the window sill and continued at 10-inch intervals up to eye level. Such a structure (which can be made entirely of wood, or of metal or wood with glass shelves) can be good-looking and help solve the problem of growing a lot of plants in a small space. It also has the advantage of keeping the plants farther from the glass than shelves attached directly to the window frame or sash, thus reducing the danger of chilling in cold weather, and makes it possible more easily to manipulate curtains to provide shade when necessary.

We shall undoubtedly find, as information accumulates, that some varieties of African-violets require more illumination than others for their optimum growth. There is some evidence that the glossy-leaved varieties, such as 'Amethyst', 'Norseman', and 'Commodore', also the Du Pont strain, can stand more sun than the hairy-leaf kinds and those with Girl-type foliage. 'Double Blue Boy' seems to be very susceptible to too much light.

ARTIFICIAL LIGHT

Some amateurs have solved the light problem by growing their plants entirely by artificial light. One, Fay Stillwell, reporting in the *African Violet Magazine,* used two 40-watt fluorescent tubes, with an automatic switch to give alternating twelve hours of light and twelve hours of darkness. The plants were set 2½ feet, 3¼ feet, and 4 feet from the lights. This, while it promoted good growth, resulted in overlong petioles and no blooms. By increasing the number of lighted hours per day to fourteen, the plants nearest the lights started to bloom followed later, though not so profusely, by those farther from the source of illumination. After twelve months another fixture using three 40-watt tubes was installed.

Lawrence C. Koehler, writing in *The Home Garden,* tells of his cellar room 15×5 feet, painted with white enamel and lighted by twelve 40-watt fluorescent tubes and twelve 20-watt tubes. He grows more than 500 saintpaulia plants disposed on two tiers of shelves along the walls of the room. The lights are turned on for ten hours each day, but the shelves are set only 15 inches from the tubes; this, plus the non-light-absorbing walls and ceiling, doubtless supplies more light to the plants than the Stillwell setup. Mr. Koehler, who has grown saintpaulias for many years by orthodox methods, claims better results in his artificially lighted cellar plant room. Richard F. Stinson, who held a research fellowship established by the African Violet Society at Ohio State University, reporting at the 1951 Convention, indicated that when plants were grown under only artificial illumination, best results were obtained by using 40-watt cool white or daylight fluorescent lights furnishing 300 foot-candles when installed 11 inches above the pot rims. These were in operation for twelve hours each day.

Another point in connection with aspect and its corollary light intensity is that it was formerly generally believed that a relatively dim light is desirable for immature plants and that when they reach flowering size more light is needed to induce free blooming. One of the large wholesale growers of saintpaulias figured on growing the young plants in a relatively dark house with illumination equal to about 400 to 600 foot-candles. Then, when they had made some growth, they were spaced out to allow better air circulation around them and given from 600 to 1,000 foot-candles. Now it seems on the basis of experimental work carried out by Richard F. Stinson, that between 900 and 1,100 foot-candles (readings taken at twelve noon) is the most desirable light intensity for growth *and* bloom under greenhouse conditions.

Another commercial grower uses double- or triple-tier benches with the young plants in the lower bunks. Here, on a cloudy day, about 50 foot-candles were registered near the edge and 30 foot-candles a foot in; while the top bench gets 1,000 or more foot-candles. A reading I made at 9 A.M. on an overcast day in May gave 1,000 foot-candles. It must go much higher than this on a sunny day, and some varieties, notably 'Double Blue Boy', were showing bad effects.

Now there is a minor mystery in this connection. I suppose that most amateur enthusiasts are able to grow, and flower, their saintpaulias with a much lower light intensity than the commercial growers. In my own case, using a photo exposure meter with masks designed to measure incident light at high-illumination levels I find that at noon on a cloudy day in mid-April I get only 30 foot-candles on my bookshelf and 600 foot-candles in the bay window. Early in May, on a sunny but hazy day, I get 80 foot-candles on the shelf and 800 foot-candles in the bay, with higher readings, naturally, in a few spots where, transitorily, the sun was shining unobscured by the shading curtains and trees. These spots have given readings as high as 4,000 foot-candles but never for more than a half hour or so at a time—longer periods than this would almost certainly result in injury to the plants.

To Sum Up: Undiluted sunshine in general should be avoided except, possibly, during the short days of winter in northern regions. The aim should be to provide enough light to induce flowering without injury to foliage. Always remember, though, that it is not enough to provide optimum conditions in one respect alone. If you remove one leg from a three-legged stool it does not make a satisfactory seat; similarly, when growing saintpaulias, if one of the factors necessary for success is lacking—soil, fertilizer, temperature, correct watering, light, humidity, or freedom from pests—the cultural structure has an uneasy balance and is likely to topple over.

LIGHT GARDENS

The most efficient way to grow symmetrical floriferous saintpaulias is under fluorescent lamps, since the light is constant and even the plants make steady growth without the danger of sunburn or growth-inhibiting dim days. Light gardens in the basement or spare room are now the standard growing system for serious growers of saintpaulias. Light-garden fixtures are available

African-violets thrive under three 40-watt fluorescent lamps in this light garden designed to fit on a wall. The lamps are hidden by a wedged louver. Mirrors on the wall behind the plants have been added to double beauty and reflect light back into the foliage.

in sizes ranging from a small single-lamp 20-watt free-standing unit to multi-tier efficiently designed light-garden carts that hold hundreds of plants.

Decorative Types In a living room, office, or similar living space, select a decorative light garden such as the furniture models with concealed fluorescent lamps. Several firms offer cabinets, sideboards, and end tables, in different designs, all with built-in fixtures and waterproof trays specifically created to combine the convenience of furniture with the beauty of growing plants. The Marko company offers a unique shelf garden that combines a wooden waterproof tray (treated with clear plastic resin inside) and an overhead fixture with a plastic wedged louver that hides the fluorescent lamps from view. The wedged louvers let light shine directly on the plants below but prevent distracting glare. Sturdy brackets fasten the two parts to a wall, turning ordinary space into a continually changing work of living art.

Free-standing fixtures with two 20-watt or two 40-watt lamps are practical when used on flat surfaces such as a large shelf, sideboard, or table. Place pots on top of moist gravel inside a waterproof plastic or custom-made wooden tray, directly under the fixture. This arrangement is efficient for growing but less decorative than lights in custom-designed garden furniture and the Marko wall gardens. In limited space such as for a desk or in the kitchen, choose one of the circular plant growth lights that use a circline Wide Spectrum Gro-Lux lamp. Several saint-paulias will fit in each of these units. The light is sufficient for maintenance over a period of several months or all year long if the plants also receive some sunlight.

Hours   To save energy you can set an automatic timer to leave the lights on for twelve to fourteen hours per twenty-four-hour

African-violet 'Rhapsodie Ophelia' (left) and 'Rhapsodie Sophia' (right) thrive under a 22-watt circline lamp in a sturdy tabletop light unit. At center is miniature Sinningia 'Dollbaby'. Moist gravel under pots provides extra humidity.

This light-garden unit comes as a quickly assembled kit, complete with two 20-watt horticultural fluorescent lamps. The unit has a waterproof tray, perfect to help maintain humidity around indoor plants.

period. You can also use fluorescent light to supplement sunlight. For example, if your plants only receive a few hours of sunlight each day, not enough to have them bloom abundantly, supplement the daylight with ten or more hours of fluorescent light. Providing more than eighteen hours of light per twenty-four-hour period only wastes energy.

How Bright? Watch your plants carefully to determine how they are reacting to the fluorescent light. If the leaves grow tightly and foliage is yellowish, the lamps can be farther away. When foliage has long stems, reaches upward, and blooms are sparse, the light should be more intense.

Fertilizer Remember that saintpaulias grown under fluorescent lights have no cloudy days so they need a constant supply of moisture and fertilizer. For example, plants on a coffee table in diffuse daylight may only need water every week and fertilizer every month, while a similar plant grown in a light garden with fourteen-hour days will need water every few days and fertilizer every week for maximum flowering.

As in all growing situations it is better to use dilute fertilizer often, rather than strong fertilizer less frequently. Dilute chemical fertilizer to ¼ strength and apply in solution at least every other watering.

More Details For an in-depth coverage of light gardening, including plans for custom-designed units, and an extensive discussion of companion plants, consult *The Complete Book of Houseplants Under Lights* by Charles Marden Fitch.

TEMPERATURE AND HUMIDITY

The ideal temperature for saintpaulias during the months when artificial heat is necessary is between 65° and 70°. They can endure and indeed enjoy higher temperatures than this but not when combined with dry air. *We must remember that temperature and humidity are linked*—the higher the temperature of the air, the greater its capacity for holding water vapor.

In homes that are centrally heated, the air becomes excessively dry unless water is evaporated in considerable quantity (about a gallon a room every day) to supply the increased capacity of the air for holding moisture. Therefore, in our homes, when the heat is on, it is desirable to allow the temperature to drop somewhat below the ideal during cold, dry weather when the furnace is running full blast, unless it is possible by measures to be described later to keep the relative humidity up to at least 50 per cent. In the bay window of my study, filled with saintpaulias, during the winter months the temperature at night frequently falls to 50° and on several occasions has dropped to 45°; during the day, with the sun shining through the windows, the temperature may rise to 75°. All this with no apparent damage to the plants. It seems to me that saintpaulias can endure quite low temperatures *provided* they are not suddenly chilled, not exposed to cold drafts, and the day temperature rises to 70° or so to average things up. So don't be deterred from growing them because the temperature of your home occasionally drops to 50°.

The areas in which the progenitors of our modern African-violets are found wild are characterized by high humidity. Now, although saintpaulias are amazingly adaptable to conditions which are vastly different from those of their native habitats, the maintenance of a fairly moist air (at least 50 per cent humidity) is important for best results. Thus, in climates where artificial

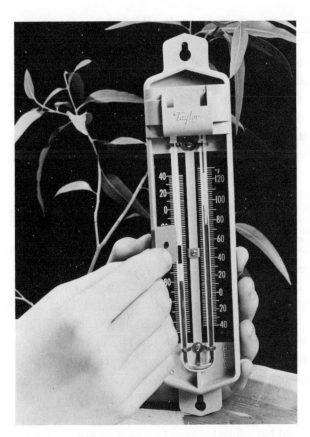

Use a maximum-minimum thermometer to check lowest and highest temperatures around your home. A small magnet resets the indicators after each reading (left).

heat is required to keep our rooms at the 70° to 75° temperature considered necessary for our comfort, it is desirable during
the winter to put into use various means for increasing the
amount of moisture in the air. If you doubt that the air of your
home is any drier in winter than it is in summer, consider for a
moment those closet doors which fit loosely during the winter
and cannot be closed in summer because the wood has swollen,
owing to the moisture absorbed from the air.

HOW TO MAKE THE AIR HUMID

When your home is heated by a hot-air system and the furnace is
equipped with a humidifying device which is kept supplied with
water (very necessary, this!), you are well along in the battle
against dry air. If the heating is by steam or hot-water radiators,
evaporating pans kept constantly filled with water stood on, or
suspended alongside, the radiators (these can be purchased) will
help to a considerable extent. Even more moisture is needed,
however, during those cold, dry days when the furnace is running at full blast. Fortunately it is not too difficult to supply
extra humidity if you are in earnest about it.

A good way to moisten the air in the vicinity of the plants is to
make use of watertight trays (in which water is kept) filled with
pebbles on which the pots are stood. These can be broiler trays,
shallow baking pans, hamburger trays (at least that was the
name given them by the salesman in the hardware store), or
trays sold solely for the purpose. These last are about 27×7
inches, made of aluminum, and are supplied with brackets which
permit their attachment to window sills. I have had satisfactory
results from them when raised about an inch above the radiator
covers of a hot-water system using fin convectors. Whether the
plants could be injured if stood in such a tray over a steam radiator I do not know. I imagine, however, that if the tray was kept
from direct contact with the radiator by a layer of asbestos or
similar insulating material, and the heat waves deflected by some

A 22-watt plant growth lamp is a suitable showplace for African-violet hybrids, here shown with companion phalaenopsis orchid and a miniature begonia.

African-violets and companion tropical plants grow in this light garden cart under 40-watt fluorescent lamps.

'Ballet Dolly', a hybrid with contrasting colors in its abundant flowers.

'Ballet Heidi', with glowing pink single flowers.

'Ballet Ulli' is typical of modern Saintpaulia hybrids bred for rich color, vigor, and abundant flowers.

'Candy Lips Improved', a floriferous double hybrid.

'Cordelia', a vigorous variegated hybrid.

'Coral Caper' shows the new shades appearing in modern hybrids.

means from the foliage, the plants would not suffer. I do know that they can endure the heat of a hot-water radiator for a couple of weeks.

Whenever circumstances permit, it is desirable to have a tinsmith make a tray, 1 inch deep, to fit the available space, which obviates the makeshift appearance of hamburger trays and the like. The larger the tray, the more effective is its performance. The one constructed for my bay window is 7½ feet long by 2½ feet at the widest part. Just to convince myself that it really helped to moisten the air I brought our "humidiguide" from the hall where it registered 40 per cent humidity and placed it on the plant bench where the pointer came to rest at 75 per cent. Even on my desk six feet away it registered about twenty points higher than in the hall.

The pebbles used in the trays should be placed to a depth of ¾ inch and should not be less than ⅛ or more than ⅜ inch in diameter. I like very much the granite chips, sold as chicken grits by the local feed store. These average about ¼ inch, are of a pleasing gray color, and absorb water which greatly magnifies the area from which moisture can evaporate. I suggest that you purchase a 100-pound bag, which is more than enough to provide a ¾-inch layer spread over about 20 square feet of bench and window-sill trays. If you are unable to obtain chicken grits you may be able to get crushed oyster shells which have the advantage of absorbing only a little light; or the gravel used for surfacing tarred roofs may be obtained from a firm dealing in builders' supplies. Coarse perlite is also useful.

Among the supplementary measures that help maintain moisture in the air are growing lots of plants and using ordinary porous pots rather than the impervious plastic or glass ones. Plants transpire a great deal of moisture mostly through their stomata (breathing pores) and water vapor rises from the soil contained in the pots. Moisture also evaporates from the sides of the porous clay pots which is the reason why, other things being equal, it is necessary to water the soil more often than when it is contained in impervious pots.

Far be it from me to suggest the abandonment of the washing machine and a return to the old-fashioned way of doing laundry at home. I merely point out that in less-enlightened days the clouds of water vapor arising from the wash boiler and the open washtub were effective humidifiers and fairly constant—when there was a baby or two in the household.

TERRARIUMS FOR SAINTPAULIAS

It is very much worthwhile, for our own benefit as well as for that of the plants, to change that Death Valley atmosphere characteristic of many apartments and homes. But if the foregoing measures for doing so seem too onerous or for any reason impractical, there is another way of providing high humidity in the vicinity of the plants by making use of terrariums, which are, essentially, miniature greenhouses intended for use within a dwelling. If you are unable to locate one in a store near you, an aquarium can easily be adapted to serve the same purpose. All that is needed is a layer of pebbles to place in the bottom on which to stand the pots, and, in some cases, a glass cover.

The size is dependent on circumstances and the number of plants it is desired to accommodate. My own ex-aquarium is 8 inches wide by 22 inches long by 9 inches high—large enough to hold three plants of medium size. Ordinarily a smaller size than this is not desirable; but when an individual plant or a number of seedlings or plantlets are to be cared for, an ordinary fish bowl, provided it is at least 9 inches across, will serve.

The layer of pebbles can be about an inch deep and ½ inch of water should be kept in the bottom at all times when the air is dry. Whether or not it is desirable to provide a glass cover depends on the aridity of the room and the area of the case. I find that the side walls alone of my ex-aquarium (even though it stands on a hot-water radiator) are enough to confine the moist air needed for the growth of saintpaulias and various kinds of

Miniature African-violets are quite at home in terrariums. This charming landscape was created by hobbyist Sally Freedman, using suitable tropical companion plants such as dwarf Ferns, Begonias, and other types that thrive under terrarium conditions.

softwood cuttings. If, however, the area of the terrarium is much in excess of 2 square feet, the walls alone may not be able to keep the air sufficiently humid in the vicinity of the plants. In such a case a pane of glass should be cut a little larger than the area of the terrarium to make a cover which will rest on the side and end walls. A close fit is not necessary or desirable, for it would keep the air within the case completely saturated with moisture which would condense on the glass and obscure one's view of the plants. If the glass should fog up it can be controlled by tilting the cover with the help of a small wood block, or by sliding it partly off to leave a ½-inch opening.

Charming miniature vistas and landscapes can be created inside larger terrariums by planting miniature saintpaulia hybrids with dwarf Ferns, and other suitable tropical companions.

CHAPTER 3

Soils

Saintpaulias are successfully grown in a wide variety of soil mixtures, but it is important they should have the right texture or
physical condition. The rooting medium must be well-aerated
and therefore light and porous. Except when the plants are fed
entirely by nutrient solutions, it should consist of about half mineral soil (loam, sand, vermiculite) and half decayed organic
matter (leafmold, sedge peat, rotted manure, compost). Saintpaulias are fairly tolerant to soil reaction and will grow in acid
to slightly alkaline soils. I had a batch of three dozen seedlings

*As an experiment, some African-violet seedlings were planted
in a window box in either strongly acid or slightly alkaline
soil. Eventually those in the alkaline soil made slightly more
vigorous growth.*

growing in a window box one half of which contained soil with a reaction of pH5 (strongly acid), the other half pH7.5 (slightly alkaline). For a time no difference could be discerned in the growth of the plants, but finally those in the alkaline half grew a little more vigorously. Although soil reaction is not too important it is advisable to avoid extremes. It is generally believed that a slightly acid soil (pH6.5 to pH6.9) is preferable and this is in accord with my experience.

HOW TO MAKE A GOOD SOIL MIXTURE

The simplest kind of mixture to fill the conditions outlined above, the "makings" of which are available to most gardeners consists of one part each of garden soil and coarse sand (or vermiculite) and two parts of organic matter which can be flaky leafmold, or sedge peat, or peat moss, or a mixture of one or more of these and *rotted* manure. If the soil is clayey and sticky, increase the amount of sand and/or vermiculite; if your base soil is on the alkaline side, use peat moss in preference to leafmold; if it is acid, add 1 tablespoonful of pulverized dolomite limestone to each peck of mixture. After the plants have been potted a few weeks, test the soil; sprinkle the surface with limestone if it is still too acid. (Sufficiently accurate test kits to determine acidity and alkalinity are available at most seed stores.) If leafmold, sedge peat, or rotted manure is not available, use peat moss to supply the organic matter and add ¼ cup of bonemeal to each peck of mixture. I got along for years without sterilizing the potting soil used for African-violets, but in order to help avoid trouble from crown rot, mites, thrips, and nematodes it is advisable to sterilize the soil (and pots) before using. For seedlings which are harmed by a rich mixture, use equal parts of sand, soil, and peat moss.

Many saintpaulia dealers sell potting soil ready mixed and sterilized, thus affording a source of supply for those who have no easy access to the "makin's" and for those who have no time to bother with soil preparation. Although the price of soil may make you think of the cost of real estate in the more expensive sections of Manhattan, it is a convenience not too costly for busy people, and I suspect that in most cases the dealer, while he does not lose anything on the transaction, does not make an exorbitant profit—not when you figure the cost of mixing, sterilizing, packaging, and mailing.

OTHER SOIL MIXTURES

The published recipes for African-violet soils include as many (or more) ingredients as there are in clam chowder. Among the bulky elements noted are clay soil, loam, garden soil, sandy soil, woods soil, soil scraped from beneath a hedge; Oak leafmold, Redwood leafmold, black spongy leafmold, and just plain leafmold; peat moss, sedge peat, Georgia peat, humus peat (muck?), compost, rotted manure (horse, cow), dried manure (cattle); sand, vermiculite.

Among the items used in comparatively small proportions are charcoal, crushed oyster shells, bonemeal, superphosphate (½ pound of 20 per cent to 1 bushel), chicken manure, and sheep manure.

Here are a half-dozen of the mixtures which have been used and recommended by amateur and commercial growers. You will notice that, for the most part, they add up to the same thing —approximately half mineral, half organic. They are included to indicate the variety of materials that can be used to attain this end. The desirability of using animal manures and fertilizers is determined largely by the nature of a garden soil or loam—if it is inherently rich they could well be left out and material less rich in plant foods substituted—peat moss and leafmold.

Mixture 1:   2 parts loam, 1 part vermiculite, 1 part Oak leafmold, 1 part poultry manure with peat moss litter (six to seven years old), 1 part muck, a handful of bonemeal to each bushel; crushed oyster shells used for drainage material in pots.

These plantlets were all grown from a single leaf. Now the plantlets are ready for transplanting into small pots of pasteurized mix. Hardwood charcoal (top right) and unmilled sphagnum moss (top center) are used in the bottom of each pot, over gravel or chards.

Mixture 2:   4 parts garden soil, 2 parts sand, 5 parts leafmold, 1 part dried cattle manure.

Mixture 3:   4 parts loam, 4 parts leafmold, 2 parts sand, 2 parts dried manure, ½ cup bonemeal, 2 cups broken charcoal (¼ inch and smaller) to each peck of mixture. The last item is not essential, but does help make the mixture light and well-aerated.

Mixture 4:   5 parts loam, 2 parts sand, 3 parts vermiculite, 9 parts leafmold, ½ part bonemeal, ½ part charcoal.

Mixture 5:   1 part garden soil, 1 part sand, 1 part leafmold, 1 part peat moss, 1 part dried cattle manure, ½ part charcoal.

Mixture 6:   1 part sand, 1 part leafmold, 1 part rotted manure.

Parts are by measure—not by weight. A flowerpot of suitable size—2 to 6 inches, in accordance with the total amount to be mixed—is a good measuring tool. Loam is soil containing approximately equal parts of clay, silt, and sand; muck is sedge peat or peat moss in an advanced stage of decay so that it is powdery when dry and of a loamy consistency when wet; leafmold is rotted leaves—flaky, but crumbling easily; charcoal is broken into about ¼-inch pieces—it can be obtained already broken from most feed stores; sand should be coarse (⅟₁₆ to ⅛) and gritty; vermiculite is horticultural grade. Sift coarse material through ½-inch sieve. *For seedlings* (and young plants from cuttings): equal parts sand, leafmold, peat moss, and soil, sifted through a ¼-inch sieve.

COMPOST AND HOW TO MAKE IT

The term compost nowadays is most usually applied to a mixture mainly of raw organic materials put up in layers interspersed with a small amount of soil and used either "pure" or with other ingredients when decay of the organic materials is fairly well advanced. This is an excellent method of providing suitable potting soil, but one has to wait for six to eighteen months, depending on moisture, heat, character of materials, and frequency of turning. Most of the pile should be thoroughly decayed and the remainder should crumble readily when squeezed in the hand before using.

One successful amateur uses "pure" compost, of leaves and grass clippings laid up in layers with animal and chicken manure and some soil and allowed to remain outdoors until it has broken down into crumbly material.

The foregoing is not specific as to quantities of each ingredient, which gives me an excuse to mention, giving chapter and verse, a compost made by me in which my wife and I grew some first-class plants without any supplementary feeding. It consisted of: 6-inch layer of spoiled hay (cut in June), 2-inch layer of freshly cut grass and weeds, wood ashes (a sprinkle—just enough to see they were there), 1 inch sandy soil, 2 inches fresh horse manure.

These layers were repeated in the order given until the pile was about 3 feet high, and then covered with a 2-inch layer of soil. This was made in August, and, after one turning and mixing (during the first fall), was used eighteen months later, at which time some of the heavier material (grass stems, et cetera) was not fully decayed, thus providing the loose, well-aerated rooting medium in which saintpaulias delight.

Other Compost Ingredients   Now for "variations," as the cook-books say. Tree leaves gathered in the fall, plus weeds pulled from the garden, lawn clippings, and vegetable tops (Carrots, Beets, et cetera), could be used in place of the hay and freshly cut grass and weeds. The wood ashes, because they happened to be on hand, were used to neutralize acidity which develops as the organic material decays and inhibits the growth of desirable "breakdown" bacteria and fungi. Substitute powdered limestone if no wood ashes are available. Sandy soil is not essential (sand may be added to the finished product if necessary to make it porous); any good garden soil may be used; its purpose, like that of manure, is to inoculate the pile with micro-organisms which bring about decay, and, in the case of soil, to give a little "solid" material in the mass. The covering of soil is to help prevent loss of nutrients in gaseous form and keep the mass moist. Barnyard manure may be substituted for horse manure; or poultry or sheep manure in lesser amounts—about ¼ -inch layers.

A moderately fertile soil is all that saintpaulias need, but it must be open and well-aerated.

IMPORTANCE OF SOIL STERILIZATION

As previously mentioned, it was not my practice in the past to sterilize the soil used for saintpaulias, but since I have been growing them in great variety, the appearance of soil-borne pests, hitherto absent, indicates the desirability of sterilizing, or rather pasteurizing, the soil. Many of the troubles that affect the plants are wholly or partially soil-borne. These include nematodes (microscopic worms), earthworms, root and crown fungus diseases, thrips, mites, and annoying but not really injurious pests such as springtails and "black flies."

Soil may be treated with various chemicals to destroy certain harmful organisms, but no one of them is fully effective against both fungus and animals pests, so the home gardener had better rely on heat to do the job, especially as it usually is more convenient.

Pots (but not the plastic kind, which may warp when heated —these can be thoroughly washed with soapy water), soil, and drainage material (if of broken flowerpots or other material that has been in contact with the soil) may be treated at the same time. Prepare whatever soil mixture you are going to use, fill pots to within ¼ inch of the rims with it, except for one pot, which should contain the drainage material.

Get a large roasting pan with a fairly tight-fitting cover, or an old-fashioned wash boiler, or a large saucepan. Put ½ inch of water in the bottom with a metal or wood rack to raise the pots just above the level of the water.

Stand pots on rack, bring the water to a boil, cover the container, and keep water boiling twenty minutes for 2- to 2½-inch pots, thirty minutes for 4-inch pots, forty-five minutes for 5-inch pots.

The idea is to maintain a constant temperature of from 140° to 160° for at least twenty minutes. If you have a suitable thermometer you might put the bulb in the middle of the pot of soil farthest removed from the heat and examine it from time to time to satisfy yourself that the right degree of heat is maintained.

Better results can be obtained in half the above-time periods at 10 pounds' pressure in a pressure canner or cooker.

Another method is to put ½ inch of water in a saucepan, bring it to a boil, fill pan with soil, and simmer for 15 minutes.

The odor of soil cooking is not pleasant—I do mine on a wood fire outdoors.

Moist heat is more efficient than dry heat in destroying obnoxious organisms, and is less destructive to the structure of the soil, so the above methods are suggested in preference to the commonly recommended practice of putting the soil in a baking pan and cooking it in an oven at 180° or 200° for one hour.

Nitrates may be formed in toxic amounts when soil rich in organic matter is heated. However, two commercial growers of my acquaintance heat their soil, including the organic matter, to 180°, and say they have no trouble; but one of them, who uses chemical fertilizer, adds it *after* the soil is sterilized. It is advisable, as a safety measure, to remove the pots as soon as cooking is done and water them once or twice (so that it runs through the drainage hole) to leach out any excess nitrogen. Wait several days, or until the soil is just moist—not wet—before using it.

With so many modern potting soils available at garden stores, in clean plastic bags in many different sizes, there is really no need to struggle with the process of soil cooking. Even when you require large quantities of a potting mix you will not save much money because commercial potting formulas are available in large wholesale-size bales at moderate cost.

Seedlings Baby saintpaulias do not grow well in a rich soil—at least that has been my experience, and other growers have mentioned this also. So, in preparing soil for them I would suggest sterilizing *only* the loam, thus avoiding the danger of overloading the soil with nitrogen as a result of heating, and adding equal parts of sand and peat moss which are likely to be free from injurious organisms anyway.

Sterilization of the soil does not necessarily insure complete freedom from soil-borne troubles unless you are starting from scratch with seedlings. Sterilized soil is easily contaminated if it comes in contact with unsterilized soil. One has to take a chance of reinfection whenever new plants are acquired, but I believe most professional growers practice soil sterilization. If you sterilize your soil and still acquire soil-borne troubles, take comfort from the thought that you did your part in trying to avoid them.

MODERN POTTING MIXES

In recent years several major manufacturers have introduced professionally prepared potting mixes based on the formulas developed at Cornell University and the University of California. These potting mixes are based on peat moss combined with sand, in the case of the University of California mix, or with vermiculite and perlite, in the Cornell formulas. In addition to the basic ingredients, many contemporary formulas include varying amounts of fertilizer.

Advantages There are several advantages to using professionally prepared and packaged potting mixes. Most importantly, the best mixes are carefully blended to provide consistency from package to package. Once you establish successful growing techniques with a given formula you can count on having the potting soil remain the same from batch to batch. The professional mixes are also free of weed seeds and most are pasteurized to kill fungus spores and other troublesome organisms.

Finally, the professional mixes are blended for specific groups of plants. In the case of African-violets, you will find several formulas labeled specifically for saintpaulias. In other cases, a general mix is labeled as being suitable for plants which need a humus-type formula, with slightly acid reaction, such as African-violets.

By using professionally prepared potting mixes, you avoid having to bake ingredients, search for several different materials, test for acidity, worry about pests in the soil, and find storage space. Since the commercial mixes come in different-size packages, you can buy what you need when you need it.

Nationally Available The best mixes are available at garden stores, supermarkets, and through mail-order catalogues on a national basis. Some of the popular formulas suitable for African-violets are Black Magic, based on a soil-free formula of leaf-mold, peat moss, perlite, and fine charcoal; Burpee mixes, all soil-free blends of peat moss, perlite, and vermiculite; Jiffy Mix, a peat-lite-type potting formula based on shredded sphagnum peat moss and vermiculite; Terra-Lite African-violet soil, based on peat moss and vermiculite with a slight quantity of perlite for added drainage; and Vita Bark African-violet soil, a university formula of composted bark, peat moss, and sand.

In addition to mixes sold in consumer-size packages, there are some suitable commercial formulas offered in large bags and bales. These include Ball Growing Mix, Metro Mix, and Pro Mix. These are generally available through wholesale supply houses that sell to nurserymen. Buying potting mixes in large bales lowers the per-pot cost but you must have some place to store the big packages. The timed-release fertilizer granules, mentioned in the next chapter, are a good means of providing fertilizer for African-violets grown in the new soil-free formulas.

CHAPTER 4

Fertilizers

First-class plants of African-violet can be grown without supplementary applications of fertilizer provided they were potted originally in good soil. My wife has a couple of plants of 'Blue Boy' that I potted for her in pure compost made as described in the preceding chapter. These, nearly two years later, were in good condition, still blooming without having had even a smidgen of fertilizer. They outdid themselves with many flowers 1⅞ to 2 inches across. And yet saintpaulis do respond to fertilizer if they are in need of feeding.

To satisfy my wife, who was inclined to doubt the value of fertilizer, I took a couple of plants in 3-inch pots, same variety, same size, same soil, put them side by side on a window tray, and gave one of them a weekly dose of liquid fertilizer. Its effect was apparent in a few weeks in stronger growth and more and larger flowers than its neighbor.

Newly potted plants (if they are in soil and not a sterile medium such as vermiculite) do not need, nor is it desirable to use, added fertilizer until the roots begin to crowd in the soil—which may be a matter of four or five months. Start with half the strength recommended, making an application about every four weeks. If the result is favorable, bring the solution up to normal strength and use it every two weeks; but stop at the first sign of unfavorable reaction and flush the soil with clear water to remove excess of fertilizer salts.

FOOD IN LIQUID FORM

Liquid fertilizer can be made from animal manures or chemical fertilizers; often these may be used alternately to advantage to supplement each other. Liquid animal manures are smelly, less convenient to make, and the percentage of phosphorus contained in them is low in comparison with that of nitrogen and potash. However, if your soil is deficient in organic matter (though it should not be) it might be desirable to use one or other of the formulas (see below), using animal manures in the hope that, in addition to nutrients, it will provide growth-regulating substances such as vitamin B_1, which may be lacking in some soils.

Mention of vitamin B_1 is a reminder that some amateur growers believe they get excellent results from dissolving the

African-violet 'Ballet Abby', a pure white hybrid, shows much better growth with regular fertilizer in this test conducted by Charles Marden Fitch. All plants started as same-size propagations and were grown under the same conditions in a light garden. Regular feeding is more important than the brand of balanced house-plant fertilizer used.

tablets in prescribed amounts and occasionally watering the plants with the solution. But soil scientists tell us that though vitamin B_1 is essential for plant growth, it is unnecessary to use vitamin pills under good soil conditions because it is synthesized by micro-organisms working on organic matter in the soil, and under normal conditions plants make it in their leaves. Because of this and because of comparative experiments I carried out with added vitamin B_1 on a variety of potted plants with negative results, I have not thought it worthwhile to try it on saintpaulias growing in soil. I did, however, apply it to a pot of leaf cuttings in vermiculite. A similar but untreated pot produced only half the number of plantlets as the one which was given the vitamin. Some commercial products, such as SuperThrive, contain vitamin B_1.

LIQUID MANURE FROM ANIMAL FERTILIZER

A pat to a pail is one recommendation for making manure water of the right dilution, but the size of the pats is not uniform, thus the liquor may vary in its strength. Another is to dilute to the color of weak tea, but one's weakness is another's strength, so the advice is still not sufficiently explicit. Here are some formulas gathered hither and yon which are a little more definite and may be more helpful than the vague directions above, even though the quality of the ingredient may cause variation in the end product.

Cattle manure (fresh or rotted): 2 quarts to 3 gallons of water.

Cattle manure (dried and shredded): 1 quart to 2 gallons of water.

Sheep manure: 1 quart to 2½ gallons of water.

Poultry manure: 1 pint to 2 gallons of water.

(*These are for stock solutions. Dilute with equal amounts of water before application.*)

The living room is not the best place to make the brew—select a place where the odor will not disturb non-gardening occupants of the house. I would suggest the use of boiling water to kill insect eggs and immature larvae when making the stock solutions from undried manures. Allow the manure to steep for at least a week before using, and stir daily. If the manure is contained in a coarse mesh bag (which is desirable if the original product is coarse in texture), push and pommel it with a thick stick to squeeze out the goodness. A stone crock is a good container.

Easier to mix and much more pleasant to deal with is liquid fish emulsion and similar organic matter processed especially for plant fertilizing.

Plants whose roots fill the pots may be watered with manure water every two to five weeks during the active growing season. The soil in the pots should be moist, not dry, when it is applied.

LIQUID MANURE FROM CHEMICALS

For many, the simplest and most convenient way of making a liquid fertilizer is to use an ordinary "complete" garden fertilizer with an analysis of 5 per cent nitrogen, 10 per cent phosphoric acid and 5 per cent potash; or a 4-12-4; or, if you believe (as many do) that saintpaulias have a high potash requirement, a "potato" fertilizer with an analysis of 5-10-10. These may be used at the rate of 1 teaspoonful (level) to 1 quart of water. Apply when the soil is moist—not dry—as in all cases when using liquid nutrients.

Almost every piece of literature dealing with the feeding of saintpaulias recommends one or more proprietary brands of fertilizer. I have no doubt that the fertilizer named was effective for the one who used and recommended it, but it is no assurance that it will be the best for your soil which, for example, may contain an ample supply of the most prominent element in the recommended fertilizer. The proprietary brands of fertilizer sold for home use vary greatly in the proportions of major elements —nitrogen, phosphorus, and potash—contained in them. For example, I have three brands in my desk drawer. *Number 1* contains 8 per cent nitrogen, 16 per cent phosphoric acid, and 7 per cent potash, plus minor elements. *Number 2* contains 7 per cent nitrogen, 6 per cent phosphoric acid, and 19 per cent potash, plus vitamin B_1. *Number 3* contains 23 per cent nitrogen, 21 per cent phosphoric acid, and 17 per cent potash.

If your soil is lacking in all the major elements, Number 1 or a similar formula (in which the major elements are in the ratio 1–2–1, generally considered a well-balanced fertilizer for most purposes) might be best to use; if the soil is low in potash, Number 2 would be preferable; while Number 3 is preferable if nitrogen is lacking.

COMPENSATING FOR FOOD DEFICIENCIES

Which fertilizer element is most needed? One way to get an inkling is to have the soil analyzed, which you may be able to persuade your State Agricultural Experiment Station to do; or you could do it yourself, less accurately and completely perhaps, with the aid of a soil-testing kit which can be bought at moderate cost.

Another way is to try to diagnose what is lacking from the appearance of the plants, which is not by any means an exact or sure method but is better than none. So far I have not come across any work detailing the deficiency symptoms in saintpaulias, but on the basis of the pattern in other plants that have been investigated, and my own observations, this is the way I would proceed.

Acid or Alkaline?   First check the physical condition of the soil in regard to porosity and drainage, then test for reaction to find out if it is too acid or alkaline. Maybe the correction of faults in these directions is more important than adding fertilizer which might do more harm than good if the soil is poorly aerated from lack of porosity or waterlogging, or too acid or alkaline.

Nitrogen? Then, if the leaves have an over-all yellowish cast, and the condition is not caused by too much sun, I would assume that nitrogen is in short supply and make use of liquid animal manure, or a chemical fertilizer rich in nitrogen along the lines of Number 3.

Phosphorus? If growth is good but the plant constantly refuses to bloom and its failure cannot be attributed to insufficient light, or to the presence of cooking gas, I would guess that phosphorus is needed and stir a teaspoonful of 20 per cent superphosphate in a quart of water and use it occasionally, or a fertilizer rich in phosphorus, such as 4-12-4.

Potassium If the leaves are yellow toward their edges, and especially if the edges turn brown, there is a possibility that potash is needed, in which case Number 2, or the "potato" fertilizer (5-10-10), would help. If there are no definite symptoms except that the pot is crowded with roots and the plant is growing slowly and the flowers are small for the variety, the general purpose 5-10-5, or Number 1, is indicated.

There is nothing certain about this method, but I have followed it with my own plants with some success, so I pass it along. In connection with it there is one important thing to remember: saintpaulias tend to have a rhythm of growth and rest; toward the end of their growth period the flowers are likely to be smaller than normal. It is not wise to give fertilizer during this slack period, but rather when they are, or should be, actively growing.

TIMED-RELEASE FERTILIZERS

Fertilizer in timed-release granules will supply nutrients to your plants over a period of months. Most of the popular brands have

Timed-release fertilizer pellets release a controlled quantity of nutrients over a period of months.

a plastic coating or similar method of holding back the fertilizer so that it is released only in the presence of water and higher temperatures. As temperatures drop and the soil becomes drier, the fertilizer pellets release fewer nutrients. With increased water and higher temperatures, both part of an active plant's environment, more nutrients are released to feed the active plant.

Nationally available brands suitable for African-violets include Osmocote (14-14-14), MagAmp (7-40-6), Ortho African Violet Food (6-9-5), and Precise Timed Release African Violet Food (8-11-5).

Use these timed-release products according to package instructions. If you wish to include a water-soluble fertilizer in your growing program, in addition to the slowly released products, then use no more than half the recommended quantity of any timed-release granules. As with otner fertilizers, package numbers refer to the fertilizer formula, always in the same order, to show the percentages of nitrogen, phosphorus, and potassium in each product.

GROWING IN NUTRIENT SOLUTIONS

Saintpaulias may be grown with their roots directly in nutrient solution contained, preferably, in an opaque vessel. This method, however, sometimes presents the difficulty of providing adequate support for the top, so I much prefer to use a sterile medium such as vermiculite or sand (or a mixture of the two) to anchor the roots and support the plant. To avoid root injury and to insure an even distribution of roots throughout the rooting medium, it is desirable to use young plantlets taken from the propagating bed and transferred directly to pots 3 to 4 inches in diameter, in which they are to grow to maturity.

The nutrients may be conducted to the roots by standing the pot in a saucer filled with the solution; but a better method, because it is less time-consuming, is to use wick-watered pots with a reservoir to hold the solution. (See Chapter 6.)

If you enjoy playing around with chemicals and like to mix things up, you can prepare your own nutrient solution as follows: 1 teaspoonful of nitrate of soda, 2 teaspoonfuls of super-phosphate, 3 teaspoonfuls of Epsom salts, 1 teaspoonful of muriate of potash, 5 gallons of water. Shake up the ingredients separately in about a pint of water. After it settles, pour off the clear liquid from each jar into a 5-gallon container and fill up with water. Certain minor elements are needed by plants in very small quantities. Usually these are in fertilizer grade chemicals, but to make sure 1 teaspoonful (half the usual rate) of trace element stock solution, made up as follows, may be added to 5 gallons of culture solution: ½ teaspoonful of ferrous sulphate, ¼ teaspoonful of boric acid, ¼ teaspoonful of manganese sulphate, ¼ teaspoonful of zinc sulphate, and 1 pint of water.

Most of us, because of the time-saving element, prefer to use one of the many brands of soluble complete fertilizers sold in small packages in florist, drug, and hardware stores. Since these vary a great deal in the proportions of the various nutrients contained in them, I throw out the suggestion to those of my readers who like to experiment that it would be interesting, and helpful in giving a line on the fertilizer requirements of saintpaulia, to grow a number of plants of the same size and variety in different solutions. The complete formula I chose had an analysis of 8 per cent nitrogen, 16 per cent phosphoric acid, and 7 per cent potash, plus thirteen other elements in varying percentages. The solution was made up according to the directions on the container. Everything went well for a time, but it appeared later that there was too great a build-up of fertilizer salts in the rooting medium so I reduced the strength and frequency of application as told in detail in Chapter 7 (efflorescence disease).

It is necessary to watch closely the behavior of the plants and govern procedures accordingly. If they grow well at first and then begin to look unhealthy, it may mean that they are getting too much of a good thing, especially if a white efflorescence appears on the surface of the soil and the sides and rims of the pots. The remedy is to flush the medium from above, several times, in quick succession, with clear water. Then dilute the solution one half and replenish the reservoir with water once or twice between each use of nutrient solution. In any case it is desirable to apply water from above every two or three weeks to leach out any toxic materials that may be present; and I think it a good plan to start off with a solution at half the strength recommended on the package—you can increase the strength if pale leaves and feeble growth indicate starvation.

Growing saintpaulias in this way has definite possibilities, especially for those who have difficulty in obtaining suitable soil. One advantage in using a sterile rooting medium such as vermiculite is that one is free from nematodes and similar ills—provided that a start is made with clean plants.

CHAPTER 5

Pots and Potting

Saintpaulias are not deep-rooting, so when containers more than
4 inches in diameter are used, dwarf kinds—either 5- or 6-inch
bulb pans or 5-inch ¾ pots (Azalea pots)—are preferred. They
will bloom in 2¼-inch pots but 3- to 4-inch pots are desirable
for plants of good size; only in the case of exceptionally large
specimens is it necessary or desirable to go beyond the 4½-inch
size. Those whose space is limited, especially if they want to
grow a number of varieties, are advised to set a 3¼-inch limit
on pot size and raise young plants to take the place of mature
specimens which will begin to decline in vigor unless potted in
larger sizes.

POROUS VS. IMPERVIOUS POTS

Both kinds have advantages and disadvantages. The soil in
porous pots, because of evaporation of moisture through the
sides, dries out more rapidly than in non-porous kinds (glass,
plastic, glazed pottery, et cetera). This involves more frequent
attention to watering (unless watered by wick or constant-level
water. See Chapter 6). On the other hand, loss of moisture by
the evaporation does aid in making the air humid in the vicinity
of the plants. Porous pots may admit more air to the soil than

Miniature African-violets are charming planted in small glazed bonsai pots. This is medium pink-flowered 'High Stepper', a semidouble hybrid with dark green leaves.

the impervious kinds, though this is disputed by one authority. They are essential when plants are watered by a constant water-level system.

Because the soil dries out more slowly in non-porous pots, it is necessary to exercise greater care to avoid overwatering. In my opinion it is desirable to increase slightly the amount of coarse sand in the potting mixture and add a little broken charcoal to insure free drainage and aeration. I have saintpaulias growing in both kinds of pots and cannot see that one produces better plants than the other, provided the necessary cultural adjustments are made. The following considerations should be weighed in deciding whether porous or non-porous pots are used:

Aesthetics   Non-porous pots usually are better-looking and the outside of them can be kept clean with less effort.

Cost   Porous pots break more easily than those made of plastic; but glass pots and glazed pottery are just as vulnerable when dropped as the ordinary porous clay pot. Utility-grade plastic pots are lighter weight and less expensive than clay pots.

Soil   If your soil is retentive of moisture, porous pots are preferable.

Humidity   If the air of your home is not adequately moist, use of the porous kinds will help humidify it.

Having pondered all these considerations, you will probably do as I did, become an opportunist, accept whatever pots are available, and end up with all kinds, though I must say, on the whole, I prefer porous pots.

Other containers include Strawberry jars, Fern-dish liners, porous rocks, and "driftwood."

THE ART OF POTTING

Saintpaulias are difficult plants to pot up without injury when their leaves extend far beyond the diameter of the pot; especially varieties which make a tight rosette with their lower leaves

This young plant of 'Ballet Dolly', with white and blue double flowers, is thriving in a recycled margarine tub with drainage holes burned in the bottom.

spreading horizontally from the center; and the Amazon and Du Pont types whose leafstalks are stout, brittle, and unbending. Because of this it is desirable to pot them in their flowering size containers, either directly from the cutting pot or from 2¼-inch pots, before the leaves spread so widely that they are in the way. When it becomes necessary to divide and/or repot large, old plants, a certain amount of breakage is inevitable, but if the job is done with care, only the older leaves will be casualties and their loss may be beneficial in reducing the demand for moisture on an injured root system. It helps a little to avoid injury to leaves and roots when dealing with oversize plants, if their soil is on the dry side. Then the leaves are less turgid with water and in consequence more pliable, and the soil breaks apart more readily when slightly dry. If too wet, the soil may wad into a putty-like mass as a result of the kneading necessary to separate the crowns with roots attached, or to reduce the size of the soil ball.

When to Pot There is no set season for repotting; usually young plants are constantly coming along, and plants in 2- to

2½-inch pots need a shift into a larger pot whenever their roots become crowded. Old plants, already in pots of sufficient size, and which are to be given new soil in the same size pot, should be dealt with when they stop blooming and are starting new growth.

Preparing the Pots   The pots should be washed inside and out and, if they are of baked clay, sterilized by boiling. If they are new, they should be soaked in water for an hour or two. When they are dry, put a piece of broken flowerpot over the drainage hole and then a ¼-inch layer of chicken grits, limestone or bluestone chips, crushed oyster shells, or flowerpot chips, followed by a small wad of sphagnum moss. The chicken grits and crushed oyster shells—the latter supplied by poultry men to their flocks to enable them to lay hard-shelled eggs—can be obtained from feed stores; the stone chips, from a builders' supply company or a garden store; the flowerpot chips you make for your-

This is what a healthy root system looks like when plants are ready to be transferred from small 2–3-inch pots into 4–6-inch containers.

Sand, loam, and peat moss are assembled and partly mixed, usually in equal parts. A piece of broken pot covers the drainage hole to prevent clogging; flowerpot chips are in hand and about to be added on the pot bottom.

self with the aid of a hammer; and sphagnum moss—the kind used by florists for covering wreath frames—from the local florist, by raiding the cemetery dump, by getting your feet wet in a sphagnum bog, or from mail-order firms. The foregoing procedure is to insure that surplus water quickly drains out of the pot and thus minimizes the danger of waterlogging. It is to be used only when the plants are watered from above; when they are watered from below by saucer or by the constant water-level method, a single piece of flowerpot to keep soil from sifting through the drainage hole is all that is needed. For the method of potting wick-watered plants, see Chapter 6.

The potting soil should be moist—not dry, not wet; when a handful is squeezed, it should hold its shape, but break apart at the slightest touch.

Setting the Plant   When potting bare-root plants—divisions of crown or plantlets from leaf cuttings—put a little soil in the bottom of the pot; hold the plant in one hand, its roots in the pot, with the junction of roots and crown ¼ to ½ inch below the rim; and, with the other hand, pour in soil around and over the roots to fill pot to rim. Tap bottom of pot gently on the table or potting bench and then lightly press down soil with the fingers so that the soil surface is ¼ inch (2¼-inch pots) to ½ inch (3- to 4-inch pots) below the rim to allow room for watering.

A three-crowned parent plant that has been resting and, now that new growth is again starting, is in condition for dividing into three parts.

Placing the plant on its side shows where the crowns are attached to each other; a sharp knife cuts them apart.

After the cutting operation, the divisions are gently pulled apart with care to permit each one to retain its full quota of roots.

One of the divisions is centered in its new pot. Its leaves are being held aside so that soil can be put in with the other hand and lightly firmed into place.

All three divisions after potting. Despite precautions, two leaves were broken, but they can be grown into new plants.

A division only five months later.

"Potting On"   When shifting plants already in pots, first remove plant from pot by turning it upside down and tapping rim of pot on the edge of table, holding the fingers of one hand on soil ball so that it does not fall to the floor. Put enough soil, lightly pressed down, in new pot so that when the root ball is set on it the crown of the plant is ¼ to ½ inch below the pot rim; fill in soil between the old ball and the side of the pot, tap bottom of pot gently on table, and then poke a 6-inch wooden pot label into the new soil all around the pot, in between leafstalks, to insure that there are no large air spaces in the soil; tap pot on bench again and level surface soil with fingers. Saintpaulias need to be potted loosely; if the procedures outlined above are followed, the soil should be consolidated to the right degree of firmness.

When repotting is completed, or a sizable batch is done, put the plants in a convenient spot (bathtub, or floor not harmed by water) and sprinkle with lukewarm water from a watering pot with a fine rose (sprinkler) to wash all soil off the leaves and to settle the soil in the pots. Leave them in the shade, out of drafts, until leaves are dry.

This plant is removed from its pot by being turned upside down and tapping the rim on the edge of the bench. Fingers hold the soil and keep the plant from falling.

REPOTTING MATURE PLANTS

So far, reference has been to potting plants with bare roots and to those "shifted" to a pot of larger size. Sometimes, in the case of mature plants, it becomes desirable partially to change the soil because its texture has deteriorated as a result of the complete decay of the organic matter which helped to keep it open; or sometimes repotting is necessary because the plant has developed a long, ungainly stem. Repotting in these cases is a matter of turning the plant out of its pot and reducing the size of the soil ball by gently kneading it with the fingers and shaking it to remove much of the old soil, thus making it possible to repot the plant in a pot the same size or even smaller than the old one. See Chapter 7. It is not necessary to remove *all* the old soil except

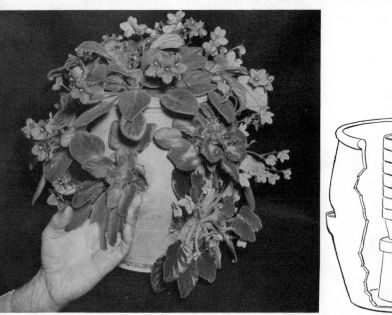
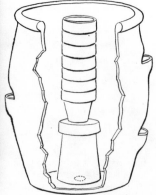

Growing African-violets in a Strawberry jar is one way to save space. The diagram at the right shows one method of providing aeration with flowerpots.

when it is extra pasty or the roots are in bad condition with the major portion dead or decayed.

Cut off any dead or decayed roots, remove a few of the lowermost leaves, and set the plant in the new pot so that the base of the crown is ½ inch below the rim; spread the roots as much as possible and try to work the new soil in between them. Press soil down gently. Water thoroughly and keep the plant shaded from the sun until the development of new leaves indicates that it is recovering from the shock of drastic disturbance.

Potting Plants to Be Watered from Below   The drainage material should be omitted when plants are watered by capillarity from below. When this is done by way of the saucer in which the pot stands, or by the constant water-level method, a piece of broken pot over the drainage hole will keep the soil from sifting through; in wick-watered plants the wick itself serves the purpose. See Chapter 6.

SAINTPAULIAS IN A STRAWBERRY JAR

Saintpaulias don't *have* to be grown in regulation pots of clay, plastic, or glass. I have already told about growing them in Ferndish liners, and in the crevices of tufa rock and in driftwood. (See Chapter 1.) Some growers are planting them in small, partially rotted logs with suitable cavities. Now for the advantages and disadvantages of growing them in a Strawberry jar. I was inspired to make this planting partly by a writer in the *African Violet Magazine* who wished someone would try it and partly because it would permit growing more plants in a given area. The jar is 12 inches deep, 8 inches across at top, has nine side openings ("cups"), in three tiers. It occupies, in table space, a circle about 15 inches across and accommodates twelve plants averaging about 10 inches across; so you see this arrangement does help overcome spatial limitations.

While saintpaulias do not require an extensive root run, they do require a well-aerated soil. It seemed desirable for cultural reasons, therefore, to reduce the bulk of soil and provide for its aeration. This was done by first putting a "Long Tom" Rose pot (two or three "nested" 2¼-inch pots could be used instead) upside down over the drainage hole in the bottom of the jar; on this a tin lid was placed, and then a column of nested 2¼-inch flowerpots high enough to reach the soil surface. The plants are watered by filling the core of empty pots to overflowing, the tin lid serving as a baffle to prevent the water from running directly through the drainage holes and out of the jar without wetting the soil. By this method the water seeps out at intervals all along the column of pots and moistens the soil evenly from top to bottom —at least I hope it does! Anyway, the vigorous growth of the plants indicates that there is nothing radically wrong with the system.

Other methods of providing a workable core will doubtless occur to many. The jar could be crocked for drainage in the usual way, and soil filled in to the lowest side openings. Then a mailing tube 2½ to 3 inches in diameter could be placed in the center to serve as a form to be filled with chicken or turkey grits, or limestone or bluestone chips, such as are used for surfacing driveways. The tube, of course, should be gradually removed as the work of planting proceeds. One of those tall, cylindrical cookie cans, about 3×8 inches, could be used as a form (cut out the bottom with a can opener) instead of a mailing tube; or it could be left in place without filling with stones if a few holes were punched in the bottom and sides to distribute water and admit air to the mass of soil. Of course it would ultimately disintegrate, but before this happens the jar will need replanting.

Planting   Because it is necessary to make the soil fairly firm to prevent future settlings, a quart or so of charcoal in about ¼-inch pieces, vermiculite, or coarse sand, should be added to your usual saintpaulia mixture to insure porosity and aeration. Fill the jar with soil up to the first tier of openings; remove the plant from the pot, insert root ball diagonally from the outside, and cover with soil—mostly from inside. Some manipulation of the root ball and perhaps addition of a little soil from the outside will be necessary to fill the "cup" and leave the surface with a slight uniform slope. The important thing is to insure that the roots are covered with soil and pressed down to eliminate large air pockets. Proceed in this way to within 2 inches of the top, then place three plants equidistant around the core and fill around them to the rim with soil.

Use Small Plants Plants from 2- or 2¼-inch pots are best; some of mine were from 3's and presented a planting problem analogous to getting a camel through the needle's eye. Remembering the brittle nature of saintpaulia's leafstalks, you will realize that gentle care is needed to do the job without injuring the plants and that slam-bang methods are "out." When planting is completed, spray leaves with tepid water to remove any spilled crumbs of soil and then give the jar a good soaking to settle the soil by filling the core with water two or three times in quick succession. Do not water again until the surface shows signs of becoming dry. I find that it is necessary to water at intervals of five to ten days, depending on weather, humidity, et cetera. Giving the jar a quarter turn every few days, if it is standing in a window, is desirable to distribute the available light equitably.

Varieties The varieties I used in the top were 'Double Blue Boy', two 'Blue Boy', 'Redhead Supreme', 'Amazon Pink', and 'My Lady Sue' in the upper tier of "cups." In the middle tier were 'Lady Geneva', 'Periwinkle', and 'Snow White'. 'Ruffles', 'Velvet', and 'Neptune' were below. This selection was made primarily to accommodate these varieties with little thought as to their suitability for the purpose. If I were to replant, several changes would be made. 'Double Blue Boy' would go because all too often the flowers open before the stalks are long enough to display them (I don't like this variety, anyway), and it just does not fit in. Its place would be taken by another 'Blue Boy'; or a clean sweep would be made and three plants of a variety with more upstanding leaves, such as 'Frieda' or 'Jessie', could be used. 'Redhead Supreme' is far too robust and already has had several leaves pruned off to keep it in bounds. For this I would substitute 'Blue Pet'; and replace 'Amazon Pink' with 'My Lady Lois', thus having one tier of varieties with Girl-type foliage. 'Pink Beauty' (or perhaps 'Dainty Maid') would be set in the middle tier in place of 'Periwinkle', which grows too vigorously. 'Ruffles', which makes a poor floral display for me, would be discarded and 'Jessie' substituted; while the one received from a grower, such as 'Velvet' (which is hardly different from 'Blue Boy') would have to give place to 'Tinted Lady', and 'Frieda' would take the place of 'Neptune'.

No matter how carefully varieties are selected, the chances are that some will find the conditions so much to their taste that they will outstrip some of their neighbors unless their leaves are subjected to an occasional pruning.

Disadvantages   In spite of pruning, some varieties will grow too vigorously and some may not make the grade, thus giving the planting an unpleasing, asymmetrical appearance. Individual, vigorous plants cannot be removed from the openings for replacements without severe root injury which might result in their death. So I suspect the best way to handle this problem is by way of a clean sweep, starting by removing the three plants in the top and, working downward, carefully loosening the soil with a kitchen fork so that the plants remaining can be pulled from the "cups" with as many roots as possible. Those that are worth saving could be potted in the usual way; then if you think well of this method of growing saintpaulias, the jar should be scrubbed inside and out with soapy water, well scalded with boiling water, and replanted with youngsters.

Nail-keg Alternative   If you are unable to obtain a pottery Strawberry jar, an ordinary nail keg (get from hardware store) may be adapted to serve the same purpose. Bore three tiers of three holes, 1 inch or so across, staggering them so that no hole

Sturdy well-designed window-sill planters with clip-on saucers are suitable for small trailing African-violets and the new miniature hybrids.

is immediately above another. Then treat the inside with Cuprinol to deter decay, paint the outside to pretty it up, let dry several days. Wash off, and proceed with planting. Because of the small size of the holes, it is desirable to use plantlets direct from the propagating medium rather than potted plants.

New Hybrids   Several recently introduced miniature and semi-miniature trailers would be perfect in a keg or Strawberry jar. For example, 'Lora Lou', 'Pixie Blue', and 'Happy Trails', all have a gradually cascading habit, quite appropriate for this style of planting.

CHAPTER 6

Watering

Saintpaulias are not bog plants even though they can survive, and apparently thrive, with the pot in which they are growing standing in an inch of water for months on end. Neither are they desert plants, though they can recover when watered after the soil has been allowed to become almost dust dry. Ideally the soil should be kept moist but never sopping wet over long periods. During the time when the plants are resting, usually in summer, particular care should be taken to avoid overwatering. The water used should be of the same temperature as the air or a few degrees warmer. So much for generalities. Let's now take a look at some of the details of *how, why,* and *wherefore.*

What Kind of Water? Traditionally, rain water is the very best that can be used for watering any kind of plant. I would advise using it if it can be conveniently obtained—*provided* it is clear and does not come from a roof fouled with sulphuric acid and other injurious chemicals from industrial plants. In other words, country rain water is first-class, free from injurious minerals, and contains nitrates in minute amounts which in a mild sort of way serve as a fertilizer.

Much city water is chlorinated heavily to render it safe for drinking. There is a widespread belief that such water is bad for saintpaulias, but I doubt if it is disastrously detrimental. There is also a belief that its use may cause a variance from normal in the color of the flowers. In these parts the town water is so redolent of chlorine, and so unpalatable, that when we eat out we first fill up on water from our own well to avoid having to quench our thirst with the chlorinated stuff. And yet good African-violets are grown in the neighborhood by those who have to use this water. Even so it cannot be beneficial, and those whose water supply is chlorinated are advised to expose it to the air for four hours or longer, or boil it, to remove the free chlorine.

Hard water also is supposed to be injurious. Our own water supply (pH7.2) from a deep well has an "eighteen-grain hardness," but we are able to grow some pretty good saintpaulias, and so far I haven't had the nerve to use the water as an alibi to account for occasional failures. When temporary hardness is present it may be precipitated by boiling and the water thus rendered softer. Perhaps an easier way of handling a hard-water situation is to use an acid medium to supply the organic matter (such as peat moss), the acid of which will combine with the alkaline elements to form relatively insoluble substances.

Water-softening devices are not always desirable. There is one process which works on the principle of exchanging sodium for the calcium and magnesium which make the water hard. While this results in water in which soap lathers freely and this is good for the hair and complexion, and for washing clothes and dishes, it may be a case of out of the frying pan and into the fire so far as plants are concerned, because sodium is more harmful to the soil than calcium and magnesium. If your water system is equipped with a water-softening device of this nature, and your plants do not thrive, it would be advisable to get water from another source for your plants.

Undoubtedly in some sections the most readily available water contains sulphur, sodium, and other matter in injurious amounts. In cases where the water is suspected, it is advisable to get it elsewhere. Usually bottled water free from injurious minerals can be purchased in those regions where the local supply is unpalatable. Rain water could be used if it is practicable to collect a clean supply; or the water obtained when the refrigerator is defrosted, though this usually is in such small amounts that it is enough for only a few special plants.

WATERING FROM ABOVE

When the plants are watered from above, a watering pot with a long spout with the tip curved downward, or a battery filler helps greatly to apply the water gently to the soil and without splashing it on the leaves. There is no real objection to water on the leaves *provided* they are not chilled by it and not exposed to the sun before the leaves are dry, but if you refrain from wetting them you are safe from this hazard. Many commercial growers water their saintpaulias with water from a hose with a sprinkler nozzle but they are careful to have the water properly tempered and to shade the plants. Even so, I have seen thousands of plants with injured leaves ("ring spot," Chapter 7) because the operator was in a hurry, became careless, and used water cold enough to chill the plants.

Whenever you do water the plants, give enough to wet the soil all through—driblets may moisten the surface soil and leave the lower half dust dry—and do not water again until the surface shows signs of becoming a little bit dry. The need for water may be determined by sight, touch, sound, and heft. Look at the soil, and water when it becomes paler in appearance; touch it, and if it feels dry, water is needed; tap the pot with your knuckles or a small wooden mallet; if it rings hollow, the soil is dry; and there are some who can tell from the weight of the pot when lifted whether or not water is needed.

When to Water   The time of watering is not too important—a dry plant should be watered regardless of the hour—but a good general rule to follow is to water only when the temperature is rising. The reasoning behind this is that if water is accidentally spilled on the leaves and the temperature falls to any extent, the evaporation of the water may reduce the temperature of the wet spots on the leaves enough to cause injury by chilling. Therefore, on the whole, it is better to do your watering in the morning so that the leaves have a chance to become dry before nightfall, which usually brings lowered temperature.

There is little danger of overwatering if the soil is porous (see preceding chapter) and the pots are thoroughly drained. This last can be attended to by putting a ¼-inch layer of flowerpot chips, chicken grits, or crushed oyster shells in the bottom of the pot. The oyster shells are especially desirable if your soil is on the acid side.

One advantage of overhead watering is that it reduces the danger of "efflorescence disease" (Chapter 7) because excess salts are washed out of the soil.

SAUCER WATERING

This is a method preferred by those who have no watertight, pebble-filled trays in which the plants stand. If plants standing in saucers are watered from above, there is danger of applying too much so that it runs through the drainage hole in the pot, overflows the saucer, and injures furniture or irritates the housekeeper who has to scurry around to find rags to mop up the mess. The saucers should be large enough to hold sufficient water to rise to the surface of the soil in the pot by capillarity. An hour or so after they are filled, any water remaining in the saucer should be poured off. There are some growers who maintain an inch or so of water in the container all the time, but this is a dangerous proceeding which, almost inevitably, ultimately results in waterlogging, lack of soil aeration, and consequent ill-health of the roots. I have done it myself on a few plants and got by for nearly a year; but trouble finally developed which almost resulted in the loss of my largest and finest plant.

Advantages of sub-irrigation as compared with surface watering are as follows: it is easy to avoid getting water on the leaves;

the soil is not compacted which may be the case when water is sloshed on the surface; because the soil is not compacted it remains permeable to air and it is thus possible to keep it wetter with less danger of injury; and, finally, one is not so likely to spill water with damage to furnishings. A single piece of broken pot covering the hole to prevent soil from sifting through is all that is needed when watering from below.

On the other hand, there is probably more likelihood of the efflorescence disease developing because the movement of water (by capillarity) is upward and when it evaporates from the surface of the soil or the pot rim it leaves a deposit of minerals which may cause trouble. This can be obviated by, periodically, say about once a month, giving a copious overhead watering. A convenient way of doing this is to put the bathroom out of commission temporarily so far as its legitimate activities are concerned, stand the plants in the tub, and spray them thoroughly with the aid of the bath hose fitted with a fine spray head. It is necessary to take care that the water is neither too hot nor too cold—just tepid. This will serve a double purpose—that of flushing excess of salts from the soil and of cleaning the leaves of dust.

WICK WATERING

This is akin to saucer watering but the water is transferred by capillarity via a wick rather than by direct contact of the soil with water. It is possible to purchase several kinds of wick-watered pots, varied in color and design and made either of glass, glazed pottery, or plastic. These consist of a pot to contain the soil, a reservoir to hold water in which the pot stands on a ledge, and a wick of woven glass to conduct the water from the reservoir to the soil. I cannot see any difference in the merits of glass and plastic so far as the welfare of the plants is concerned. Plastic pots are lighter than those of glass which are more stable because of their greater weight. On the other hand, if you inadvertently drop a glass pot, that is the end of it for practical use.

In wick watering the water is conducted to the soil by capillarity operating through a wick leading from a reservoir into the bottom of the plant pot. The system has the great merit of stabilizing the soil moisture and requiring less frequent attention.

Homemade wick-watering devices are just as good, though not so good-looking as the commercial kinds. Materials for wick-pot making are to be found in almost every household. I have a quarter-pound butter dish from a nickel-and-dime store that has been in use as a reservoir for several years. Those squat glass jars (squatty ones are preferable to tall ones because they are more stable) in which various comestibles are sold make admirable reservoirs and tin lids with a hole made in them for the passage of the wick, or preserving jar rings, can be fitted into the mouth and serve to support an ordinary clay pot above the water. Most large seed stores sell glass wicks and they sometimes are advertised in garden magazines. Any absorbent organic fabric may be used (I have on occasion used strips from my worn-out pajamas!) but it has the demerit that it rots rather quickly and has to be renewed, whereas a glass wick is practically indestructible.

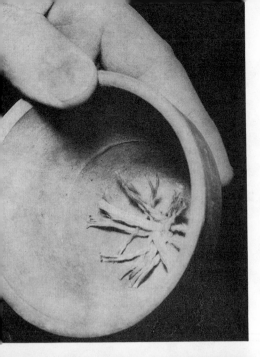

When installing a round wick, one end of it is unbraided and spread out to cover the bottom of the pot; the other end is pushed through the hole from the inside until the loosened portion comes in contact with the pot.

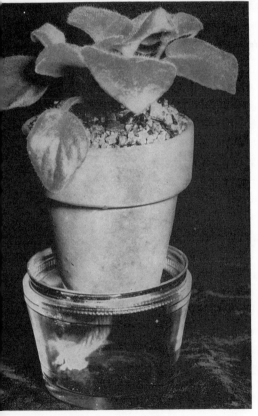

A young wick-watered plant potted in vermiculite. A clear glass reservoir enables you to see whether or not it needs refilling without moving the pot.

Special Handling   When potting plants that are to be wick-watered, one end of the wick is teased out to cover the bottom of the pot, then the wick is pushed through the drainage hole from the inside and cut off at a sufficient distance from the base of the pot to enable it to reach the bottom of the reservoir. Then pot the plant in the usual way. Ordinarily the wick closes the hole enough to prevent soil from spilling through; if it does not, just pack a few chips over the opening.

There are two ways by which the amount of water delivered to the soil can be regulated. One is to use wicks of varying thickness (partly to conform to size of pot), a matter largely of trial and error; the other is to wait a day or longer, according to the degree of wetness of the soil, before replenishing the dry reservoir. The latter method has the merit of simplicity.

One advantage possessed by the makeshift devices described and pictured for this book, quite apart from their low cost, is that it is easy to see when the reservoir needs refilling and it is not necessary to move the pot in order to do so.

THE "CONSTANT WATER LEVEL"

Some commercial growers use the "constant water-level" method for supplying moisture to the roots of saintpaulias (as well as other plants) by means of a watertight bench filled with sand into which the bases of the pots are pressed. The water level is maintained an inch below the base of the pots by a float valve attached to the water supply; it is conducted throughout the length of the bench of means of tile pipes, or by lengths of angle iron with the points of the "V" downward, and an inch or so of ¼-inch gravel. This is surfaced with an inch or more of fine sand.

This method can easily be adapted to home use. In my own home I fixed up the lower portion of a roasting pan (the top also may be used) 3½ inches deep, by putting a layer of chicken grits in the bottom surfaced by a 1½-inch layer of sand. Water

This is an example of constant water-level watering as applied to a number of separately potted plants.

is applied by way of an empty 2¼-inch pot set on the gravel at one end and filled around with sand. (*See illustration.*) The plant pots (the ordinary porous, baked-clay kind) are pressed into the sand to a depth of about ¼ inch and moisture is absorbed and carried to the soil by capillarity through the bottom and side wall of the pot. So far (I am speaking of the summer months) the soil has been kept adequately moist by occasionally pouring water into the 2¼-inch pot—putting in enough so that the level remains for an hour or more at 1 inch above the bottom of the pot, then waiting a day or two before refilling. The plants are in pot sizes varying from 2½ to 4 inches. During the winter, when artificial heat will dry out the air, and the demand for moisture by the more rapid-growing plants will be greater, I suspect that "spot-watering" of individuals from above will be necessary, if their demand for moisture cannot be satisfied by pushing the pots a little deeper into the sand.

I made use of a container that happened to be on hand. Any watertight tray 3 to 4 inches deep, with an area sufficiently large to accommodate three or more potted plants, would do; but if you want to be fancy you could have a tinsmith make a tray to fit any available space, such as a window sill.

The advantages of watering by the constant water-level method are: the soil is kept more equably moist, the humidity of the air is raised in the vicinity of the plants, and it reduces the amount of time spent in watering.

HOW OFTEN TO WATER

This is a question frequently asked, but it is one that is impossible to answer in terms of a measured amount of water every day, or every other day. The plants' need for water depends on the size of their root system in relation to the character and amount of soil in the pot; whether or not they are actively growing; the amount of light to which they are exposed; and the degree of humidity of the air.

Most of my plants are standing on pebbles contained in a watertight tray about 7½ feet by 2½ feet and they are watered from above. During the winter, when artificial heat is used, I keep the pebbles constantly moist to help maintain enough atmospheric humidity; in summer the air is sufficiently moist without this aid and the pebbles are not wet deliberately, but they do get some incidental water that runs through the drainage hole when the pots are watered.

Contrary to a popular idea that it is necessary to water more frequently during the summer, I find that the reverse is true. When artificial heat is being used I have to look over the plants every day to water those that need it; in the summer every other day is often enough, or every three days if we experience a spell of cloudy, humid weather. However, in air-conditioned rooms the lower humidity will cause the plants to dry out more often.

Week Ending   Because of the ability of saintpaulias to endure for short periods excessively wet and comparatively dry soil, they can be left without attention over a long weekend if properly prepared. In my own case, this involves filling reservoirs of wick-watered plants, putting more water than usual in the "constant water-level" roasting pan so that it comes almost to the surface of the sand (instead of 1¼ inches below), filling the saucers of the plants watered by this means an hour or two prior to the expected time of leaving and again at the last minute, thoroughly soaking the plants standing on pebble-filled trays, and then putting enough water in the trays to reach almost to the surface of the pebbles. If you are going to be away more than four or five days, it becomes a question of getting someone to come in to water the plants, of taking them with you (it has been done!), or installing a constant water-level system with an automatic float valve.

For plants growing under fluorescent lamps, set the automatic timer to supply only eight hours of light per twenty-four-hour period. The reduction of light hours causes plants to require less water.

CHAPTER 7

Trouble: Avoidance and Cure

There are numerous troubles which afflict saintpaulias that are not because of insect pests or fungus diseases but simply and solely to errors in cultivation. These can easily be avoided when you know the causes.

Ring spot is characterized by brown areas on the leaves, sometimes in rings, sometimes looking like the markings on a Chinese laundry ticket. These can be caused by cold water getting on the foliage or by sun shining on wet leaves. To avoid this trouble, use water a few degrees warmer than air temperature. Plants splashed with cold water or sprayed with insecticide or fungicide should be shaded until the leaves are dry. It is believed that some ring spots may be caused by a virus disease.

Creamy areas somewhat like variegation sometimes may occur as blotches or in a narrow band around the leaf. This may be because of overexposure to sun, in which case it can be avoided by moving the plant to more subdued light; the cause may be exposure to a cold draft; or it may be an inherent tendency toward variegation, a condition desired by some fanciers and abhorred by others. If you like variegated plants, well and good; if you don't, you can learn to like them, discard the plant, or try it in a better location, where it is not exposed to the causative factors.

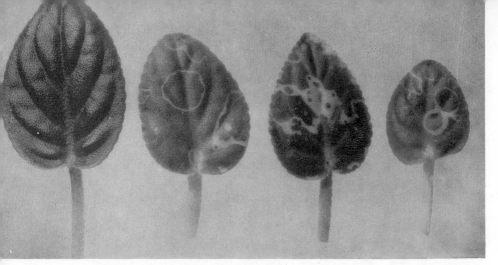

Ring spot is caused by the presence of cold water on the leaves while they are exposed to sunlight.

A somewhat similar condition develops when the plant is exposed to cold drafts of air. Blotches develop in the leaves of the plant as a result of being too close to a window during a night of gales and below-zero temperature. The injured areas at first turn a pale tan and later become creamy white as described in the preceding paragraph.

Leaf scorch is very likely to make its appearance on the leaves of plants which are exposed to undiluted sunshine after a period of dull, cloudy weather. The leaves nearest the window have mushy areas which dry out to a light brown and those farthest from the glass may have spots which look as though they were caused by leaf-spot fungi.

I had this condition affect a window box full of seedlings growing in an east window. These were shaded from direct sun by a thin curtain thumbtacked to the lower sash. For some esoteric housekeeping reason my wife removed the curtain, and as we entered a spell of cloudy, foggy weather, the curtain was not replaced. Then, suddenly, a brilliantly clear, sunny day came along and the plants, softened by a week or so of dim light, were unable to take it. By the time I thought of the exposed babies and pulled down the shade, many of the leaves had scorched edges and others looked as though they had been spattered with tan-colored paint. All my wife said was: "I told you where I put the curtain and thumbtacks!" The remedy in this case is obvious —be on the alert, especially in the spring when sunny days may follow a cloudy period, and shade the plants so they are not exposed to undiluted sun.

Yellowed or grayish foliage may be caused by overabundant light or by starvation. If the plant is growing in a small pot and is not exposed to direct sun, you can suspect the last-named cause; such plants usually respond in a few weeks to repotting in larger pots; or, if the pot is of fair size (4 inches), to the application of liquid fertilizer. If the leaves have abnormally long stalks with comparatively small blades, and the plant lacks bloom, insufficient light is the likely cause. See Chapter 2.

PETIOLE ROT

Most growers of saintpaulia are faced at some time or other with the condition commonly known as leafstalk or petiole rot which,

A case of petiole rot. The arrow points to the lesion where the stem was in contact with the pot rim.

fortunately, in most cases can be avoided by proper care. The trouble starts as an orange-brown or rust-colored lesion (depression) at the point where the petiole comes in contact with the pot rim (center of stalk of detached leaf) and often at the base of the petiole where it is in contact with the soil. Shortly thereafter the stalk shrivels and collapses.

Several theories have been advanced to account for this condition, including petiole constantly wet at point of contact with pot rim, chilling of petiole at point of contact due to lower temperature of pot as a result of evaporation, injury due to abrasion, and normal death of leaf because of age. None of these provides an entirely satisfactory explanation. A plant of 'Blue Boy,' a variety susceptible to petiole rot, in a 6½-inch pan, was mounded with sphagnum moss. Four months later it had no sign of petiole rot

A 'Blue Boy' plant was mounded with sphagnum moss and remained free of petiole rot.

in spite of the leafstalks of the lower leaves being in contact for their entire length with almost constantly wet moss which kept them moist and, presumably, chilled them just as much as a moist pot rim. A few leaves died of old age, the symptoms of which—gradual yellowing and slow withering—are quite different from those of petiole rot.

Cause It is almost universally believed now by those versed in saintpaulia culture that the cause of this trouble is chemical injury induced by the efflorescence of salts on the rim of the pot; or, sometimes, from the soil. I am convinced that this is so by the behavior of the plant I photographed. This started in life as a plantlet from a leaf cutting rooted in vermiculite. It was transferred when large enough to leave its mother to a 4-inch pot of vermiculite and wick-watered with nutrient solution made by using a proprietary, soluble fertilizer according to directions. The plant grew well for about six months, then ceased growing, and the leaves lost their healthy glow, so I substituted tap water for the nutrient solution in the reservoir. After a few weeks, growth was resumed, but enough fertilizer salts had been absorbed to cause efflorescence and the leaves in contact with the pot rim began to collapse as shown. Partly to try out a new soil-testing outfit and partly to provide some evidence that fertilizer salts were responsible I added two tiny flakes of efflorescence to 13 cubic centimeters of soil extract made from sterile sand. The sand extract, tested for nitrate, as might be expected, was negative, but when the efflorescence was added, the extract showed 250 parts of nitrate per million. (Forty p.p.m. is considered enough for good vegetative growth of plants in greenhouse soils.)

How to Avoid Petiole Rot It is easy to by-pass this form of petiole rot. In the first place, avoid overdoing the use of fertilizer, especially when it is applied from below by saucer or any method which results in the evaporation of the solution at the surface leaving there a deposit of fertilizer salts. If an encrustation of salts forms on soil or pot, flush the soil by watering heav-

Petiole rot can be averted by the use of cardboard collars cut with tabs that can be pushed into the soil to hold them.

Four months later, after being collared and having its food ration reduced, this plant was well and had lusty leaves and many flowers, although the pot was still encrusted.

ily, preferably with country rain water (as noted in Chapter 6, that collected in cities, where it may come from a sooty or greasy roof, is often detrimental), or distilled water, or low-mineral drinking water which usually can be purchased in areas where the city water is not all it might be. If you have only a few plants, you might, as suggested earlier, save and use the water collected when defrosting the refrigerator—of course waiting until it is of room temperature. This should be done several times within an hour or so to wash excess salts through the drainage hole. Then wipe off the efflorescence from the pot with a damp rag. If the rot has already made its appearance, break off all affected leaves close to the stem and put on a collar of cardboard dipped in melted paraffin, and go easy on fertilizers in the future.

The patient photographed for this discussion was collared in January, the fertilizer solution reduced to half strength, and the reservoir (a ¼-pound butter dish) filled with it only once a week, usually two fillings of tap water being used in between. Four months later it was among the healthiest plants in my collection with lush, deep green leaves and quantities of flowers though the pot was still encrusted. (This is because of my inherent aversion to dishwashing; so don't do as I don't do, but as I tell you!)

There are other methods of keeping the leafstalks from contact with the efflorescence on pot rims. One is to make a simple "guard rail" to support the leaves from two or three pipe cleaners bent at each end to form legs which are pushed into the soil, the "bar" curved to follow the pot rim. If you are not a pipe smoker, and pipe cleaners, therefore, are not at hand, you could use a strip of metal foil (tin, aluminum) to cover the pot rim— inside and out. Some who are fond of glittering surroundings cover the entire pot with metal foil anyway. Another way, applicable only when potting or repotting, is to dip the pot rim in melted *new* paraffin wax. (If "secondhand" stuff from jelly jars is used, mold may develop on vestiges of jelly in the paraffin.) I melt it down in the lid of a 1-pound tobacco can which provides the right depth for coverage. Plastic pots are much less likely to initiate petiole rot than porous clay containers.

Other Petiole Trouble In a letter, my good friend Freeman Weiss refers to the condition just discussed as "efflorescence disease," which seems to me to be a good name for it especially as there is another kind of petiole rot not apparently attributable to contact of leafstalks with fertilizer salts. This other ill is characterized by water-soaked, glassy-looking (but not glassy to touch) petioles which quickly collapse, leaving the still-green leaf blades hanging. There are probably more factors than one involved in this case. In my experience it usually is associated with a compact, poorly aerated soil and, in consequence, an unhealthy root system. This soil condition may be brought about by starting out with heavy soil insufficiently ameliorated by organic matter, sand, and/or vermiculite; by allowing the pot to stand months on end in water which causes waterlogging; by earthworms which ingest the soil and organic matter, churn it up in their gizzards, and excrete the unusable portion in a pasty, puttylike mass. Excessive use of fertilizers rich in nitrogen may be a contributing factor especially if the soil is not well-aerated. Under such conditions nitrites may be formed from the decomposition of nitrates. Nitrites in excess are known to be toxic to plants and in some cases may cause the roots to die.

CASE OF MISMANAGEMENT

The history of my oldest plant will serve to illustrate some of the foregoing points. Starting in January, two years after I got the plant, the pot was kept standing constantly in 1 inch of water and every two or three weeks was given a dose of soluble fertilizer in water. For eleven months the plant was a picture of health and continually in bloom, but in January of the third year "glassy" petioles developed on the older leaves. I suspected that an earthworm might be causing the trouble and, sure enough, when the plant was watered with lime water, a large, rosy-cheeked fellow emerged and was thrown outdoors for the birds to dispose of. The plant picked up immediately, but after a month or two the more familiar petiole rot or efflorescence disease made its appearance. A cardboard collar on the pot rim was effective, but soon there was a recurrence of glassy, gooshy, water-soaked leafstalks. Keeping the plant on the dry side by watering only when it was almost dust-dry controlled this but the plant failed to thrive. It produced no flowers and was growing smaller instead of larger, so in January of the fourth year it was turned out of its pot to find out the underlying cause of the trouble. The soil had become too compact from the loss by decay of all the coarse organic matter and the plant had very few living roots; so all the old soil was shaken off and the plant repotted in new, sandy, loose soil rich in organic matter. Water was given stingily until new growth started but the leaves were sprayed daily with lukewarm water. It began to recover right away, started blooming in March and, thirteen months later, was still going strong. Just to see what would happen, I started overwatering this same plant. Three weeks later I picked off four leaves with water-soaked stalks!

Now! It is far better to steer clear of the possible causes of "glassy" petioles than to let the condition develop and then try to cure it. Use loose, porous soil, avoid overwatering and the excessive use of fertilizer, and you are not likely to be troubled. If it does develop, and the plant does not quickly and permanently respond to less liberal watering and fertilizing, don't waste a year, as I did, in trying out palliatives, but take the drastic step of shaking the old soil from the roots and repotting the plant in new soil, half of which should be of inert material such as coarse sand and/or vermiculite to insure porosity and aeration.

There is another trouble associated with root injury caused by cultural mismanagement which manifests itself by wilting leaves without, however, any rotting of the leafstalks. This was exemplified by the lengthy stems of an ancient plant brought to me for treatment by a neighboring friend. There were several factors

Faulty root condition may lead to leaf wilting without rotting of the stems. In this case the plant was in unsuitable soil in a pot that was too large.

The unhappy plant was transferred to a bulb pan holding only half as much soil as the original pot, and the humusy soil was mounded with vermiculite

After three months in its better quarters the plant was much improved and even had a fair number of flowers.

involved here. The plant had been transferred from a 3-inch pot to a 6-inch pot (too large); an unsuitable soil had been used (lacking humus); it had been too heavily fertilized (heavy encrustation of salts around rim of pot). Also it had been exposed to too much sun which injured the leaves and reduced their demand for water. This contributed to a soggy soil condition (and injury to roots) already critical because of the large bulk of soil, uninhabited by roots, which dried too slowly.

Because of the long stems unfurnished with roots, the normal procedure of dividing the crowns was not followed. Instead, the plant was left intact (except for one crown which fell off) and repotted as low as possible in a bulb pan holding about half as much soil, of a humusy, porous mixture, as the 6-inch pot. The surface was mounded with vermiculite to cover the stems and induce the formation of roots from them.

Three months later the plant was reasonably healthy with a fair number of blooms. When the tide of blooming begins to wane, the plant should be divided, for by this time there should be enough roots produced from the stems to make the operation less hazardous.

This trouble could have been avoided by separating the crowns (instead of putting the entire plant in such a thumping great pot), potting the divisions in pots of 3-inch size (or smaller) in suitable soil, with careful attention to watering, and keeping them out of direct sunshine.

TROUBLES CAUSED BY DISEASE ORGANISMS

There seem to be no disease-causing organisms associated with the preceding, but in correspondence with Dr. Weiss concerning saintpaulia troubles he mentions a crown and root rot accompanied by petiole collapse caused by a fungus (*Phytophthora*). He isolated the organism from the leafstalks and it proved to be fatal to healthy plants . . . "attacking and destroying the root systems of leaf cuttings in water within a few days. . . . Plants attacked by it always die regardless of treatment." Dr. Weiss goes on to say: "This (glassiness and slow collapse of leafstalks) also has been reputed to be one of the symptoms of nematode injury to the roots of *Saintpaulia*. . . ."

Here is another case. One of my seedlings began to wilt, in spite of the soil being adequately wet, and exhibited symptoms similar to petiole rot except that there was no "glassiness" and the flowers also were affected—small in size, premature withering, and, finally, collapse of the petioles.

When the plant was turned out of the pot it was seen that the root system was practically destroyed; and a cut through the stem disclosed that the center was dark brown in color and rotten. The upper part of the crown, which was not discolored and seemed not to be affected, was cut off and inserted as a cutting (it died—perhaps because it had already been invaded by the fungus) as was a seemingly healthy leaf. The latter, two and a half months later, is alive and new plantlets are showing at the

A well-developed case of crown rot.

base of the stalk. The obviously diseased material was sent to Dr. Weiss for diagnosis; and the pot, soil, and paper containing it were put on a hot open-fireplace fire as a sanitary measure.

Of this specimen Dr. Weiss reports: "It appears to be a case of Verticillium wilt, and the first time I have seen this disease in *Saintpaulia*. There is no record of it in our plant disease file either. . . . Verticillium wilt is a frequent disease of certain vegetable crops and some ornamentals. As the fungus is internal and more or less systemic, no external treatment would cure it. One might perhaps get healthy leaf cuttings from an affected plant if the fungus had not spread too far." Later Dr. Weiss said: "I'll have to revise this a little. I got a Verticillium from this plant but I couldn't make it wilt other plants. I also got a Fusarium—another frequent cause of wilt and root rot. I may have emphasized the Verticillium too much, and am now inclined to suspect the Fusarium too. At any rate this appears to be a real parasitic disease—a root rot and vascular wilt."

The underground evidences of crown rot. Stems have been cut off to disclose the dark brown rotted center.

The soil in which this plant was growing had not been sterilized and one can imagine that the sclerotia or spores of the fungus were present in the soil, waiting until the plant's resistance was lowered (as it was) by careless overwatering. The fact that a leaf cutting produced healthy plantlets supports Dr. Weiss's supposition that this might be a possible way of salvaging an affected specimen.

Then there is a condition described by Regina and Warren Gottschall in the *African Violet Magazine* (Vol. II, No. 1) in which the petiole starts to rot where it joins the crown which, with the roots, was whole and healthy. The trouble was checked by removing the lower leaves and "painting" the stem thus exposed with Fermate applied with a camel's-hair brush. I have a couple of plants, 'Ruffles' and 'Blue Girl Supreme', which exhibited similar symptoms. I cut off the affected leaves close to the stem and dusted the wounds with Fermate 10 per cent, sulphur 90 per cent, and have had no further trouble.

Of this Dr. Weiss says: "This is almost certainly *Rhizoctonia* canker or stem rot. I have seen it, too, and found this fungus present. It isn't very pathogenic (disease causing), and it may only follow some injury such as efflorescence. The fact that it can be cured by a mild fungicide like Fermate also suggests *Rhizoctonia,* but I think that Arasan (which is used for brown patch and *Rhizoctonia* rot on Lettuce) would be better than Fermate."

Another possible treatment is to water the plant with Fermate, 2 tablespoons to 1 gallon of water, plus ⅓ teaspoon of mild detergent, applying it so as to wet the stem and leaf bases as well as drenching the soil. I tried this with successful results on a plant of the variety 'Waterlily', suspected of affliction with stem rot. It might be useful, too, in cases of trouble associated with Phytophthora.

There is no need for the home cultivator to become unduly alarmed about these diseases. I have grown a number of saintpaulias and so far have lost only a few plants whose demise can definitely be attributed to disease. One could be reasonably sure of being free of them if the potting soil is habitually sterilized and one gets a start with healthy stock. For the rest, follow the cultural recommendations to avoid similar troubles of nonparasitic origin noted earlier in this chapter. As added insurance, use only pasteurized ("sterilized") potting soils, such as the commercially prepared peat-lite mixtures.

NEMATODES

Nematodes are tiny worms, the males of which commonly look like eels, hence their common name "eelworm." Some of them are microscopic; others, though small, can be seen with sharp eyes. Some species are beneficial, living on harmful insects; some attack animals, and some feed on decaying organic matter—the so-called scavengers. There are several hundred species which are parasitic on plants, these for the most part being from $\frac{1}{64}$ to $\frac{1}{25}$ of an inch long. The one most commonly found attacking saintpaulias is the root-knot nematode.

Nematodes injure the plants by causing knots, galls, or swellings on the roots, thus inhibiting their proper functioning (root-knot nematode); or by causing decay of roots (meadow nematode); and sometimes are responsible for lesions or brownish blotches on the leaves. It would seem that attacks by nematodes, by weakening the plants, make them more vulnerable to attack by disease-causing organisms.

Symptoms   Evidences of nematode attacks are not well-defined and often simulate those brought about by improper culture or by attacks of fungus organisms. The sick plant which was pho-

The plant at the left is perfectly healthy. The one at the right has been heavily attacked by nematodes or eelworms.

A case of root knotting caused by nematodes. Later the plant developed swellings near the bases of several leafstalks which may have been caused by these minute pests.

tographed in this connection from surface indications could have had its troubles caused by waterlogged or unsuitable soil, or by too much fertilizer, or by crown rot. Actually the Division of Nematology of the U. S. Department of Agriculture found that "the roots were extensively knotted due to infection by root-knot nematodes. . . ." In the soil surrounding the roots, numerous specimens were found of a species which causes galls on leaves, stems, et cetera, and a few meadow nematodes. The plant was also suffering from crown rot!

On the other hand, the first sign that all was not well with a plant of 'Tinted Lady' was the small, distorted flowers produced on very short stalks barely emerging from the crown. Digging into the surface soil with tweezers, I was able to pull out a root with a "knot" on it which I assumed was circumstantial evidence of nematode attack; later, tumors or swellings developed near the bases of several leafstalks. I examined one of these under my inadequate microscope and found creatures which looked like nematodes but, not being a nematologist, I cannot say whether they were responsible for the swellings.

In general, limp, dull-looking leaves, with or without brown water-soaked dead areas, and aborted flower stalks, should make one suspect the presence of nematodes.

What to Do?   The only sure way of finding out whether or not a plant is attacked by nematodes is to send plant and soil to a nematologist who knows his business. Competent men are usually to be found in State or Federal Departments of Agriculture; but it would be better to find out whether or not a nematologist is on the staff, and whether your plant will be well received, before going to the trouble of packing, wrapping, and sending it.

If for any reason you cannot or do not wish to follow this procedure, the first step should be to isolate all suspected plants. Although nematodes in general are slow travelers, it is possible for them to move from pot to pot if plants are standing on moist sand or peat moss in a tray or bench; or if they are watered in common in a "watering trough" such as a baking pan. The chief way, however, by which nematodes are spread in saintpaulia collections is by using infested soil for potting. This at once suggests the desirability of sterilizing all potting soil (and pots) and taking special care in the disposition of soil which has contained infested plants.

The next step is to spread a newspaper over the workbench, turn plant out of its pot onto the paper, loosen and shake off the soil so that the roots may be examined. If they are swollen and knotted, they are probably infested with nematodes and the best thing to do is to put newspaper, plant, and soil in a hot fire. Boil pot and saucer if they are the pottery or glass kind (if plastic, wash thoroughly with hot, soapy water), and wash your hands. Even though no knots are visible on the roots, nematodes may still be the culprits; but if you are of a hopeful disposition, you could take a chance and repot in new soil. Keep the plant isolated and dispose of the old soil, pot, and saucer as suggested above.

Another way of dealing with suspects is to raise new plants by cutting off the healthiest-looking leaves an inch below the blade and inserting them as cuttings in sterile media. This should be done *before* turning the plant out of its pot to avoid getting contaminated soil on the cutting. Then deal with old plant, soil, and pot as previously described. The plants derived by this means should be kept away from the general collection until it is certain that they are free from nematodes as evidenced by healthy, vigorous growth.

Neil C. and Mary J. Miller apparently were successful in ridding their large collection of saintpaulias of nematodes by immersing the pots and plants to above crown level in a solution of parathion, as recorded in two issues of the *African Violet Magazine. But parathion is so dangerous to handle that its use is not recommended for the amateur and it is sold only to commercial growers.* Until the nematologists come along with a compound which is less dangerous (of which there are good prospects) it would be better to stick to sanitation and discarding affected plants. Sometimes healthy plants can be raised from an infested specimen by leaf cuttings free from nematodes.

MILDEW

I believe mildew seldom bothers African-violets. I saw it for the first time on the flowers of 'Double Blue Boy'; a little later it made its appearance on the petals, flower, and leafstalks of 'Blue Boy Supreme'. These were plants received a week or so earlier from a commercial grower.

Mildew shows up as a grayish, frosty-looking, fuzzy patch, quickly spreading on petals, leafstalks, and flower stems. It is important to get rid of it before it becomes thoroughly established. The method I followed with my incipient infection was to dust the affected areas with dusting sulphur in the following manner: A small swab of lambs' wool (snipped from a powder puff belonging to my wife) was fastened in the small loop of a paper clip and the rest of the clip straightened to form a handle. The swab was dipped in a saucer of dusting sulphur, the surplus dust removed by tapping the swab on the saucer's rim, and then the patches of mildew were gently brushed with the swab. I've had no trouble from mildew since. Lest I be accused of unscientific reasoning, I hasten to say that I had no checks and admit that the disease could have disappeared without any treatment!

In the case of a bad infestation of many plants, the method of dealing with it suggested above would consume too much time and probably be ineffective. Therefore, under such circumstances I would suggest spraying with wettable sulphur (sold under a variety of trade names) at the rate of 1 tablespoonful to 1 gallon of water—or follow manufacturer's recommendation if it says on the label to use a smaller quantity. Commercial lime-sulphur, 1 part to 200 parts of water, which leaves a scarcely visible spray residue, will get rid of mildew (two applications may be necessary) and probably is not injurious to saintpaulia. One level tablespoonful of dry lime-sulphur to 2 gallons of water will give a 1–200 dilution. The newer systemic fungicide Benlate, offered as a powder to be mixed with water, is also effective.

MITES—THE WORST PESTS OF ALL

These are among the most fearsome of all saintpaulia pests and every endeavor should be made to circumvent them. They cause distortion of leaves and flowers and ultimately, if they are not controlled, the death of the plant. There are two species commonly involved—the Cyclamen, or pallid mite, and the broad mite. Of the two, the Cyclamen mite is more to be feared because it is extremely difficult to clean up an infestation without the aid of deadly poisons which the average amateur is loath to bring into his home.

Signs and Symptoms Injury by Cyclamen mites usually occurs chiefly on the young leaves in the crown of the plant. The older leaves may have a normal appearance, but the young leaves are crowded together, dwarfed, misshapen, hard, more brittle than usual, and their edges usually curl upward. The crown has an excessively hairy appearance with the hairs seemingly pointing in almost every direction and, when viewed under a strong lens, giving the impression of a pile of jackstraws. The petioles of middle-aged leaves may be unnaturally curved and sometimes the surface is marked with brown corky tissue.

Often the first indication of the presence of mites is an unusual pale or pinkish appearance of the leaf blades at the point of junction with the stalk. But if the plant is in a flowering stage, the first noticed sign that all is not well is quite likely to be an unnatural curvature and swelling of the flower stalks, with small, misshapen flowers with discolored petals; or their failure to develop beyond the bud stage. Later, the flower stalks become

Mites usually injure the young leaves in the plant's crown. Stalks of middle-aged leaves may be unnaturally curved and show a pinkish color where they join the leaves. Notice the normal appearance of the older leaves.

A close-up view of the injury to plants caused by mites. Note abnormally curving stalks and misshapen flowers.

twisted, fail to elongate, and finally they are completely suppressed. Sometimes the flowers only are affected. In such cases I am convinced that they should be removed and destroyed by burning because of the difficulty of reaching the pest with a spray; and because if selenate is used, as described later in the chapter, its translocation to the flowers seems to be delayed.

The creature (it is not a true insect but belongs in a class along with spiders, scorpions, and ticks) which causes all this trouble is tiny, less than $\frac{1}{100}$ inch long, white in larval stage, white to brownish in adult, and is invisible to the unaided human eye. I am constantly amazed at the amount of damage that can be perpetrated by only a few of these small beasts. It would seem that they must inject a poisonous, irritating substance into the sap analogous to that injected into animals by feeding mosquitoes and chiggers.

It is necessary to use a lens with a magnification of at least ten times in order to see them; and even then it is sometimes difficult to find the little brutes because of their colorless appearance and habit of hiding in crevices and folds of the leaves and in among the hairs. Often I have found it necessary to watch closely for several minutes at a time before being able to discern any mites on an obviously infested plant. I find it is helpful to stir them up by scratching among the hairs with the head of a pin—it is easier to see them when they are moving.

The broad mite is somewhat smaller and broader and is more active. It usually feeds on the lower surface of the leaves and causes them to pucker downward.

EXPERIENCE AND EXPERIMENT

I am going to recite my own experience with these pests because it may parallel your own and may provide a little enlightenment. I had grown saintpaulias for a number of years on a small scale but when the idea of this book was broached I started assembling a sizable collection. For a long time I was free from trouble, except for minor ones such as mildew, aphids, efflorescence disease, and petiole rot, which can be controlled or by-passed fairly easily, and I was beginning to worry lest all my information concerning mite injury would have to be obtained second-hand.

Then I noticed that a plant of 'Myrtle' and one labeled 'Pink Beauty' (it is not this variety, but so far is unidentifiable) purchased two months earlier from an amateur professional were not developing normally. The flower stalks were twisted, in the case of the alleged pink variety, and the full quota of petals failed to unfurl. The flower stalks of 'Myrtle' just sulked around the crown and did not grow more than about 1 inch. For a week or so I thought to myself, "This is just a happenstance or an idiosyncrasy of these particular varieties"—which was reprehensible for one who ought to be on the alert to investigate abnormalities.

Then it suddenly occurred to me that this might be what I had been waiting for all these months—an infestation of mites. So I got busy, and by dint of much squinting and squirming, and some mild profanity, I was able to discover some moving critters (two or three) which I definitely decided were mites. But which kind? These aging eyes, plus lack of training in this kind of work, and perhaps unsuitable magnifying equipment, made it impossible for me to decide. The congested crowns, malformed, excessively hairy young leaves, distorted flower stalks and flowers, pointed to Cyclamen mites as the culprits; but the fact that no trouble was apparent during the cool season, when Cyclamen mites are supposed to be most active (broad mites are reputed to reproduce at a greater rate when the temperature is high), that some leaves of 'Pink Beauty' were puckered downward, and some of the creatures I located were sprinting along at a great rate, suggested the presence of the broad mite. Authorities tell us that both species may commonly infest the same plant, and my guess is that is what happened in my case. (I later sent specimens of what I thought to be Cyclamen mites to Dr. Smith, U.S.D.A. Entomologist, and also to Dr. Blauvelt, Entomologist at Cornell University, who confirmed my diagnosis.)

My next step was to move the two plants to an isolation ward (the bathroom), start treatments, and resolve to keep my eyes peeled to note any deviation from normal on the part of the rest of the collection. The plant of 'Myrtle' was watered with sodium selenate, chlordane, and fertilizer (a sort of shotgun prescription —selenium to control mites, chlordane to knock out soil insects such as springtails and maggots, with a mild dose of fertilizer to act as a tonic!) according to the directions on the package obtained from a dealer specializing in saintpaulias. The other plant whose symptoms more nearly approached those caused by broad mite was dusted with sulphur, which, to this species, is deadly. Then I washed my hands thoroughly and proceeded to my daily chores, prepared to wait a few weeks for results.

Two months later both plants were making new growth, and repeated search with a hand lens failed to disclose any mites.

In the meantime, six weeks after the first infestation was discovered, 'Dainty Maid' (same source) was seen to be infested; also 'Ruffles', and 'Purple Prince' from another source; and a little later 'Norseman', 'Helen Wilson', 'Sailor Girl' (flowers only) were definitely infested and, in addition, there were about a dozen suspects. All of these could have been contaminated from 'Myrtle' by way of the spout of the watering can, my hands or clothing, when caring for them.

At first, being desirous of having plenty of infested stock to observe and experiment with, I was not too careful to prevent their spread, but now the time had arrived to really get after the little beasts. Except for six plants, including 'Violet Beauty', 'Bicolor', 'Blue Eyes', 'America', and a couple of Du Pont varieties (which were segregated in the living room for treatment by spraying), the soil of all was treated with sodium selenate. This was done with some reluctance, having in mind the extremely poisonous nature of the selenate, of which more will be said later. The plants were divided into two batches: one being treated with the combination of selenate, chlordane, and fertilizer (which contains the selenate at half usual strength and requires two applications with four weeks intervening), and the other with the normal dosage of sodium selenate. At the expiration of a month, there were still some living mites on a few plants given the half-strength solution and on one plant ('Frieda') which had a full dose. 'Frieda' was sprayed with a miticide, the second treatment of selenate-chlordane solution was given, and now, three months after the first treatment, the infestation appears to be eliminated.

An infested plant of 'White Lady' was put outdoors in a shaded coldframe in June. It was given two dustings with a 1 per cent rotenone dust and there were no mites visible when it was brought indoors in September, but the plant was not in good shape. It so happened that the coldframe was situated near the potting shed where the duster was filled for use in the vegetable garden and on both occasions got a full blast of dust which was spilled in the nozzle so that the plant was half-smothered. I don't recommend this method—it is too disfiguring.

The remaining infested plants were sprayed with the dangerous-to-use TEPP (tetraethyl pyrophosphate). Eighteen days later active mites were found on the variety 'America' so all plants were again sprayed, this time with Di (p-chlorophenyl)-methyl carbinol (Dimite). Four weeks later living mites were found working in the flowers of 'Du Pont No. 1', so all six were again sprayed with Dimite. The purpose of using two preparations was to get a line on their efficacy as miticides and their effect on flowers and foliage. Dimite seems to be a slightly more effective "killer," perhaps because it has a longer residual effect than TEPP. The flowers of 'Du Pont No. 1' were marred by TEPP but not those of 'Violet Beauty'. Dimite injured all flowers with which it came in contact. Some injury to young leaves occurred (notably to 'Bicolor') as a result of the Dimite spray. The spraying was done outdoors in the shade when the temperature was above 60°; the plants were left outdoors until the foliage was dry.

In those cases where the infestation seems to be confined to the flowers, I believe it to be desirable, in view of the fact that the mites are hidden and difficult to reach anyway, to remove and burn them—not forgetting to wash the hands immediately after. Any leaves that are killed or badly malformed as a result of mite injury should be cut off and burned.

CONCLUSIONS AND SUGGESTIONS

Cyclamen mites and, to a lesser degree, broad mites, are so destructive and difficult to get rid of that it is worthwhile to take considerable pains to avoid contaminating a clean collection. To this end, newly purchased plants should be segregated at least 18 inches from other plants, preferably in another room, for two or three months before mingling them with the main collection. Do not allow your clothing to come in contact with them and wash your hands thoroughly with soap and water after tending them. Use a separate watering pot for the suspected plants or dip its spout in boiling water before using it for watering healthy plants. Omit the practice of brushing the leaves to remove dust, which is a potent way of transferring mites from one plant to another.

Other Mite Hosts Some plants belonging to other genera but commonly grown in homes also are subject to attack by mites. Among them are wax begonia, *Cyclamen, Fuchsia,* Chinese hibiscus, *Impatiens, Lantana,* and *Pelargonium* (ivy-leaf and house geraniums). If your interest is primarily in saintpaulias, you may want to consider the desirability of eliminating these other plants from your home lest they be carriers; or at least to keep them under suspicious observation.

Among the outdoor plants and some grown in greenhouses for cut flowers which may be attacked by Cyclamen mites and which may be brought into the house for decorative purposes with the mites riding along are chrysanthemums, dahlias, delphiniums, gerberias, petunias, and snapdragons. Avoid using any of these where they might come in contact with saintpaulias unless you are sure they are above suspicion, and wash your hands after making your arrangement before handling African-violets.

Because of the fact that almost irreparable injury to the plant occurs in a bad infestation and because it is much more difficult to clear up a bad infestation than a mild one, it is essential to keep a close watch on the plants to notice any abnormalities and take immediate measures to eliminate the trouble. The most desirable measures to use depend on the circumstances.

WHAT KIND OF TREATMENT?

If a careful survey shows that only one or two plants are affected, the best plan would be to put the plants, pots, and soil in the fire, wash your hands, and hope that there may be no stray mites on the remaining plants.

Non-poisonous Sprays If many plants are stricken, your attitude toward the use of deadly poisons will be the determining factor in a course of procedure. Insecticides and miticides in which rotenone is the chief killing agent, and which are practically harmless to people and pets, can be used. If faithfully applied, they will keep the infestation in check but it is not certain that they will entirely eliminate it.

Because the mites operate in crevices and among the congested hairs, it is difficult to reach them even with the aid of an efficient sprayer. Therefore, in the case of an initial infestation, it is desirable completely to immerse the plants in a lukewarm solution (follow dilution directions on the container) once every five to seven days for about fifteen to twenty-one days, and then follow up by spraying the crowns every two or three weeks as a prophylactic measure. The flowers are likely to be marred by the solution so, unless the mites are attacking the flowers, the spray should be directed into the crown of the plant to avoid getting it on them so far as is possible. Many growers believe it is desirable to spray every three or four weeks, even though plants seem to be healthy, as a preventive measure.

Hot Water Then there is the hot-water bath treatment recommended by Dr. Floyd F. Smith, Senior Entomologist of the U. S. Department of Agriculture. This requires complete immersion of plant, pot, and soil in water held at exactly 110° for fifteen minutes. Here are the directions as received from Dr. Smith:

"The following suggestions may be helpful in successfully treating saintpaulias that are infested with Cyclamen mites where the homeowner lacks special equipment. However, the treatment should not be undertaken without an accurate thermometer that is easy to read and that is calibrated in degrees Fahrenheit. A glass chemical thermometer is available from most drug companies and chemical supply houses.

"If the plants are large and they are deeply set in the soil, removal of the surface layer to expose the crowns will permit more ready penetration of heat. The plants are not removed from the pots for immersion in the water bath.

"A small number of plants can be treated in a laundry tub or other vessel if deep enough to permit covering the plants with water. Fill the vessel with water to the desired depth and adjust the temperature to about 111° F. Fill another vessel with water adjusted to a temperature of about 120° F. This water will be poured into the tub as needed to maintain the desired treating temperature of 110° F.

"Set the infested plants in the tub of water in an upright position and see that all foliage is below the surface. If several plants are to be treated, they can be set in a wire basket or tray from certain cooking utensils or in a shallow slatted box. As the water cools, pour in the warmer water to maintain the treating temperature at 110° F. for the full treating period. More hot water will be needed during the first part of the treating period or until the soil has been warmed. Remove the plants promptly after fifteen minutes, allow to drain, and set out of direct sunlight for about twenty-four hours, then return them to their usual position.

"The temperature of the water during treatment should be carefully controlled since too warm water will injure the plants and too cool water will not kill the mites. The hot water should not be poured directly on the plants in the treating vessel but at one side. The water should be agitated by stirring with a paddle to maintain a uniform temperature throughout the vessel. If the treatment is made in a warm room with no cold drafts, there will be less heat loss from the treating bath and less need for adding hot water.

"It is advisable to make a preliminary trial run without plants in order to become familiar with the quantity of hot water needed to maintain the temperature and other procedures necessary to make the treatment a success.

"Precautions should be taken to prevent reinfestation of treated plants. The mites can be picked up on the fingers when handling infested plants. The mites will move to adjacent plants if foliage touches. Many plants other than saintpaulia will harbor mites."

Mrs. Neil C. Miller, in the *African Violet Magazine* (Vol. II, No. 3) gives a detailed report of her experiences with the hot-water treatment which in her case did not give entirely satis-factory results. It is only fair to record that Mrs. Miller did not remove the surface soil from the larger pots as recommended by Dr. Smith. I have not tried this method, being intimidated by its time-consuming and laborious aspects when nothing better than ordinary household facilities are available. This attitude was confirmed in conversation with Mrs. Miller, who spoke feelingly of her exhaustion after spending fourteen hours straight in bath-ing her large collection of saintpaulias.

Poisonous Sprays   For those who have no objection to the use of decidedly poisonous preparations, there are HETP (hexaethyl tetraphosphate) and TEPP (tetraethyl pyrophosphate). These are probably more efficient killers of mites than the "non-poisonous" sprays or rotenone already mentioned but *they are poisonous, need care in handling* (they may be injurious in con-tact with the skin), and, because their vapor, if inhaled, is injuri-ous, *should be applied outdoors only,* which limits their use to the warm months so far as saintpaulias are concerned. Dimite, while it is harmful if inhaled, taken internally, or allowed to come in repeated or prolonged contact with the skin, is less dan-gerous to use than the preceding. It is intended for use against mites and is not effective against insects.

The most effective modern treatment for mites, using a prod-uct available to the home owner, is a Kelthane spray. Apply Kelthane at 1½ to 2 teaspoons per gallon of water every seven days for at least three weeks in succession. Spraying with Kelthane is much easier and actually more efficient than the hot-water treatment.

SELENATION OF THE SOIL

Treatment of the soil in which the plants are growing with sodium selenate seems to be the surest and most lasting way of combating mites and also certain insect pests. *The chief objec-tion to its use is its extremely poisonous nature.* Selenium is the cause of the "alkali disease" of cattle which results in loss of hair and hoofs, liver lesions, and edema; frequently with death as the final outcome. It occurs in areas of low rainfall (20 inches or less a year); in regions of high rainfall it seems that selenium is leached out to below the toxic limit. Soils containing one part of selenium per million may produce herbage toxic to animals that feed on it. Saintpaulias growing in selenated soil absorb enough selenium to poison the mites and some insects which feed on them.

Because of government regulations it is difficult to obtain sodium selenate and in fact its use is often highly restricted.

Safeguards In view of the poisonous nature of selenium, anyone using it should take every precaution to avoid accidents. The poison itself and any stock solution left over should be clearly labeled "Poison," locked up away from irresponsible persons, and kept where there is no danger of it coming in contact with food. Any vessels used in preparing and applying the solution should be washed after use and also the hands of the user. Leaves removed from treated plants should be buried; discarded, treated soil (from dead plants, for example) should be disposed of by spreading it thinly outdoors well away from the vegetable garden. I don't know how much selenium can be absorbed by a saintpaulia, but in view of a tentative estimate on the part of one of the manufacturers of sodium selenate that "a daily intake of one milligram of food selenium is probably not harmful to an adult," from which one might imply that only a little more might be injurious, one would be justified in preventing children and pets from browsing on the leaves of treated plants.

Many saintpaulia growers, amateur and commercial, use selenate to control mites and, so far, I have not heard of any accident or injury resulting from the practice. If, after reading the preceding paragraph, you feel that you are willing to take a chance, this is how selenium is applied.

Dosage 1 gram sodium selenate to 1 gallon of water; the solution to be used at the rate of 1 fluid ounce for a 3-inch pot, 2 ounces for a 4-inch pot.

As a guide to the amount to buy, 1 gram of sodium selenate in solution is enough to treat about sixty plants in 4-inch pots. You may have to do some shopping around in order to be able to buy it in small quantities. Several dealers in African-violets sell sodium selenate, or you might try your local druggist. There is at least one dealer who sells it in capsules in measured doses. This is a great convenience to the amateur in eliminating the necessity of weighing or measuring and reduces the hazards of spilling the poison where it might be harmful. If the selenate is obtained in a form in which the dosage has to be weighed or measured, you might be able to prevail on your druggist to weigh it out for you in 1 gram (or smaller) lots. Or you could do as I did: measure out an exact ¼ teaspoonful, not pressed down, but struck off level with a knife blade, wrap it in a piece of wax paper, take it to the druggist (with an extra piece of paper of same size to put on the weight pan of the scales) and ask him to verify the weight. Then put the selenate in a glass vessel; add a small quantity of warm water; stir, and when it is dissolved add more water and stir, or shake again. I make a stock solution of 1 gram in a ½-gallon jug and then dilute with an equal quantity of water before using.

Application   The soil in the pots should be dry enough to need watering. If you practice saucer watering, put the solution in the saucer; if overhead watering is used, be very careful to avoid wetting the leaves. As previously mentioned, the official dose is 1 ounce for 3-inch pot, 2 ounces for 4-inch pots. For measuring it, obtain a lipped graduate with fluid ounces marked on it. My own practice, however (which I don't recommend), is to put the solution in the watering can and apply it as I would in normal watering. There are some who believe that it is better to apply repeated doses at half strength, or even less. I have tried it at half strength and full strength, but the results did not allow me to come to any conclusion one way or the other.

Further Precautions   In addition to the precautions already mentioned, selenate should be applied only to plants already established in their pots. *Plants whose roots have been disturbed or injured within a month or six weeks should not be treated.* Some dealers practice selenation; and plants so treated should not be dosed again until after four or five months. Plants more than a year old are sensitive to overselenation. They should not be treated more than once a year; try to avoid an overdose.

Prognosis It takes from three to five weeks, depending on the weather and the activity of the plants, for enough selenium to be absorbed to make the sap poisonous for the mites. In the meantime they are active and causing damage, so I would suggest that it is a good plan to spray infested plants with a rotenone preparation before selenation to kill off as many mites as possible while waiting for the selenium to become effective. One treatment (of young plants) should confer immunity for about six months.

One or two of my plants died after selenation; a few showed signs of injury. It may be that some varieties are more susceptible to injury from selenium than others; it may be that my slapdash methods of application resulted in an overdose; or it may be that there were what the M.D.s call "complications"—that is, the plants may have been in a weakened condition because of crown rot, nematode attack, too much fertilizer, waterlogged soil, or anything that would cause root injury. A commercial grower of my acquaintance insists that saintpaulias infested with nematodes invariably succumb when selenated.

It takes time for plants to recover from an attack of mites and selenation. Some of mine ('Dainty Maid', 'Blue Boy', 'Amazon Blue Eyes', 'White Lady', 'Neptune') treated with selenate started to bloom again in less than three months; others were still lagging a year later. The failure to make a quick recovery can be attributed, I think, partly to summer treatment, when growth usually is less active, and partly to the severity of the infestation. In the majority of the plants treated, the original crown died, or became weakened, and numerous side crowns developed. Many of these plants will have to be divided, or pruned to limit them to one to three crowns. It would seem from the experience of others as well as my own that selenation is the answer to the menace of mites; it also is reputed to control certain insects—mealybugs, aphids, et cetera—but is not so effective against thrips. If the situation in the household is such that selenate can be used safely, I would recommend it; but, remember, a collection of saintpaulias *can* be replaced.

It is to be hoped that a systemic miticide, non-poisonous to humans may sometime be discovered.

(*Editor's Note: Since Mr. Free wrote this report on sodium selenate, the chemical has been tightly controlled by regulations and is no longer available for general use. I recommend a spray of Kelthane combined with an application of Di-Syston granules for control of mites. Apply Di-Syston according to package directions, usually about 2 rounded teaspoons per 6-inch pot. The active ingredient is absorbed by the roots and travels throughout the plant. Di-Syston is poison and must be used with care. C.M.F.*)

MEALYBUGS

Of all the insects likely to afflict saintpaulias, mealybugs are the most difficult to control. They grow to a length of about ⅕ inch. They have oval bodies surrounded by waxy filaments sticking out like the teeth of a comb. Their bodies are pink but the color is hidden by a white waxy meal. Often it is the egg sacs, looking like little wisps of cotton and containing from 300 to 600 eggs, that are first noticed. These, usually, are deposited in the angle made by leafstalk and stem, or in a leaf crevice. The insects usually prefer to feed (by piercing the plant tissue and sucking the sap) in some kind of shelter such as that afforded by the angles formed by the veins on the undersides of leaves.

Treatment If one plant only is badly infested, the cheapest and best thing to do is to put plant, pot, and soil in a fire. If several plants are attacked and the infestation is not too severe, the egg sacs can be removed by means of small cotton swabs dipped in rubbing alcohol, and the insects killed by touching them with it. This must be faithfully done every two or three days, looking over each plant very carefully, until all the insects are eliminated. When dealing with a general infestation, involving a large number of plants, spraying must be resorted to, using Isotox or Cygon 2-E, and following the directions of the manufacturer as to dilution. Put plants in the shade and spray them thoroughly; after several hours syringe them with lukewarm water and leave them in the shade for a day or two. Even so, the flowers and foliage may show some injury, but this will be of less account than that done by the insects if left uncontrolled. Cygon is useful to control soil mealbugs. Mix ½ teaspoon per gallon of warm water and drench the soil with the solution.

THRIPS

Thrips are tiny, slender insects usually less than ⅛ inch long and barely visible to the unaided eye. They are very active and agile, scurrying around at a great rate especially when they are disturbed, as, for example, when an infested flower is pulled apart. There are hundreds of species of thrips—mostly injurious, though some are reputed to feed on mites. I suspect that the greenhouse thrips and the flower thrips are the species that most commonly attack saintpaulias, though the possibility of infestation by other species is not excluded.

When leaves are infested, they are marked with numerous silvery, bleached-appearing spots and dark brown dots of excrement voided by the insects; often it is the undersurfaces that are first attacked. Thrips injury shows in the flowers by malformation accompanied by whitish streaks and brown water-soaked blotches; often the flowers are shed prematurely.

It has been suggested that the use of sterilized soil is one way of avoiding thrips, presumably because the nymphal stages in part, of some species at least, take place in or on the soil; but some species are readily air-borne and may come in through the window or over the transom when you are not looking, which, I feel sure, is the way I acquired my only experience to date with thrips on saintpaulia.

Those who are averse to the use of powerful poisons can spray or dust the plants with rotenone or pyrethrum preparations of which there are numerous proprietary brands obtainable from almost any seed or florist store. The treatment usually needs to be repeated in ten days. Use an efficient sprayer to reach the undersurface of saintpaulia leaves and the crevices of the flowers in which thrips love to congregate.

The encounter with thrips on saintpaulia, just referred to, was in connection with a healthy, vigorous, and floriferous specimen of 'Du Pont Lavender Pink' which because of its beauty had been promoted to a position of honor as the centerpiece on the dining table. One morning, as I was blithely finishing my breakfast, I glanced admiringly at saintpaulia and noticed that the newest scape of flowers was not looking quite right. The plant was hustled off to my study right away, where examination with a hand lens disclosed several active thrips operating mostly in the throats of the flowers. So I picked off the affected corollas, crushed them, and put them in the wastepaper basket to be burned, and then gave the plant a thorough spraying with chlordane (poison)—1 teaspoon of a 45 per cent emulsion to 1 quart of lukewarm water—chiefly because it happened to be conveniently handy. A few hours later I again looked over the plant and found one very groggy thrips—no sign of others, quick or dead. Ten days later I again looked the plant over in case eggs had been laid and young developed but saw no signs of thrips and none have been seen since.

The only reason for this recital is to emphasize the importance of being on the alert to discern trouble and taking immediate steps to counteract it. If this had been allowed to develop into a bad infestation, there is little doubt I would have had a tough time in getting rid of hordes of thrips. The insecticide does not harm the leaves in the least but it did cause all the older flowers to drop prematurely during the night after application, which is a small penalty if it gets rid of the pests.

APHIDS OR PLANT LICE

These are well-known mostly small but easily visible sucking insects, with, usually, pear-shaped bodies decorated by two tiny tubes standing out from the upper surface of the abdomen. Most species are easily controlled if the infestation is noticed in an early stage and immediate measures taken. The old standard remedy is nicotine and soap—1 teaspoonful 40 per cent nicotine; 1 tablespoonful soap powder, 1 gallon lukewarm water. Malathion or Isotox are modern aphid controls. Since aphids are sucking insects, it is necessary to hit them with the spray or dunk the plants in the solution.

My only experience with aphids on saintpaulias was a rather mysterious visitation which to the credulous might suggest spontaneous generation. Early in April they showed up in a window box containing thirty-six seedlings just coming into bloom. The mystery is how the pests got there. The plants were completely isolated in my bedroom from all other plants. They were set in the soil which had lain dry and idle for three years in a window box, ameliorated, just prior to planting, by a 1-inch layer of presumably sterile peat moss. It was, I thought, too early in the year for aphids to be active enough to come in from outdoors in our still wintry part of the country. But, nonetheless, there they were with no nicotine on hand. So I mixed 1 teaspoonful (level) of a powdered detergent in 1 quart of warm water, sprayed them with it and, after about twenty minutes, syringed them with clear water. Most of the aphids were killed and a second treatment ten days later cleaned up the remainder. This is related as an example of the effectiveness of a common household commodity against these easy-to-kill insects.

SPRINGTAILS AND BLACK FLIES

The springtails, which are most annoying to saintpaulia growers, belong, probably, to a harmless species which lives in, and feeds on, decaying organic matter. They are tiny, whitish, slender insects less than ⅕-inch long which hop like fleas by means of a tail-like spring when they are agitated. They often are seen in great numbers in the saucers immediately after the plants are watered.

The small black flies or gnats hovering around the plants of which so many growers complain also are more annoying than harmful, and probably originate from eggs and larvae present in the organic matter (especially manure) used in the potting mixture. My own saintpaulias have never been troubled with any of these pests so any information I can give as to their control is from other sources.

The obvious first step with pests of this nature is to decontaminate the soil used for potting by partially sterilizing it. See Chapter 3.

Many methods have been recommended for getting rid of springtails already established in the soil of growing plants, such as watering with an insecticide like Malathion, diluted as recommended on the container. For a home remedy, take plant, pot, and saucer to the kitchen sink, water thoroughly with a fine spray of lukewarm water, and when the springtails swarm in the saucer, wash them down the drain. This has the merit of being entirely harmless to the plant. Another is to put a teaspoonful of naphthalene flakes in the center of the saucer, set the pot on it, and then fill the saucer with water; but it seems to me that this might be disastrous to plants in some cases. Other prescriptions include these three: watering with 1 teaspoonful Clorox to 1 pint of warm water; with 1 teaspoonful ammonia (presumably the household kind) to 1 quart of water; or with 1 teaspoonful Lysol to 1 quart of water.

The "official" remedy is 5 per cent chlordane powder dusted lightly on the surface of the soil and in the saucer after watering.

I tried drenching leaves and soil of a plant with 45 per cent chlordane emulsion at the rate of 1 teaspoonful to 1 quart of water to find out if this would harm the plant. It didn't; and if springtails had been present, my guess is that it would have killed them.

Black flies are said to succumb to most of the above measures. However, new laws restrict chlordane use. Cygon 2-E or lindane are more practical insecticides for soil pests in the average home collection.

SUMMING UP: THREE PREVENTION POINTS

Isolate all newly acquired plants, preferably in a room by themselves, for two or three months, under close observation to make sure they are free from disease, mites, and insect pests.

Avoid bringing possible "carriers" of mites, thrips, et cetera, in proximity to saintpaulias. Take care that you yourself are not a "carrier."

Make every endeavor to provide good cultural conditions both to insure that the plants are vigorous and thus better able to resist disease, and to avoid those troubles such as ring spot, et cetera, which are not linked with fungus diseases, mites, and insects.

MODERN PESTICIDES

Keeping up to date on the best pesticides to use is not easy. Government regulatory departments, such as the Environmental Protection Agency, recommend legislation to control the sale and application of pesticides. Every few months the laws change and some state laws are stricter than the federal regulations. As of late 1977 the pesticides listed below are legally available and represent the most effective home treatment for the usual pests on saintpaulias.

Aphids: Spray first with room-temperature water under the shower or outside to remove as many aphids as possible. Then spray with malathion or a general insecticide combination such as Precise Insecticide with pyrethrin.

Mealybugs: Isotox and Cygon 2-E will control these pests.

Mites: Cyclamen, broad, and red spider mites can be controlled with specific miticides. Most effective is Kelthane. Other miticides proved useful for saintpaulias are Dimite and malathion.

Springtails and Symphylids: These soil-dwelling pests can be controlled with malathion at 1 teaspoon per gallon or lindane at ¼ teaspoon per gallon of water, used as a drench to soil, saucers, and plant trays.

Thrips: Malathion or general insecticide mixture such as Precise will kill thrips.

Whiteflies: The recently developed synthetic pyrethrin, available in Pratts Whitefly Spray, is effective against whiteflies.

Systemic Granules   In addition to the sprays listed above, pesticides can be applied to the soil as dry granules. When watered, the granules release poison which the plant roots absorb. In a day or two all parts of the plant have enough of the pesticide to kill pests that suck the sap or chew the leaves.

Di-Syston systemic insecticide granules are safe when used as directed. The control lasts for four to six weeks and is most effective against thrips and aphids but will help to control more dangerous pests such as mites and mealybugs.

Aerosol Bombs   When used at the correct distance, usually at least 1 foot away, aerosol sprays are useful for quick spot control of pests. Raid House and Garden Bug Killer spray is safe on saintpaulias and most other house plants. Remember that holding the aerosol bomb too close to plants can damage leaves since the spray is very cold when it firsts exits the nozzle.

Vapona Strips   Solid plastic strips containing Vapona insecticide are useful in controlling aphids, mealybugs, and various flying pests. An effective way to treat plants is to put the Vapona strip inside a box or big plastic bag along with infested plants. In a light garden or greenhouse, you can hang up a Vapona strip, according to package instructions, as a general preventative measure against pests. However, even with a Vapona strip hung near the plants, you should still check for pests every few weeks and spray with an appropriate pesticide if you find an infestation.

CHAPTER 8

General Care and Growing for Exhibition

Plants should not only be cleansed from dust and dirt but also must be kept free from insect and fungus pests. All-around cleanliness is important.

Dust on the Leaves This is not necessarily injurious—though it may be—but it is definitely unsightly. There are two ways whereby dust may be removed: by dry and wet methods. In the dry method, each leaf is supported gently by one hand and is brushed lightly, in the direction in which the hairs lie, by a soft-bristled brush such as is used by artists, or for cleaning phonograph records. Don't forget that in most varieties the leaves are as brittle as glass and even more fragile, and that mites can be transferred to clean plants from infested ones by means of the brush. Usually the most convenient way to remove dust by the wet method is to put the plants in the bathub, of course with the drain open, and spray them with water delivered through the bathroom hose fitted with a fine spray shampoo head. Be very careful that the water does not run too hot or too cold. If your water is hard, it might be well first to use a hand sprayer and wet the foliage with soapy water (¼ ounce of mild soap flakes dissolved in 1 quart of water) and then spray with clear water. Keep the plants in the shade until leaves are dry. This washing sometimes serves a triple purpose: it cleans plants of dust, flushes soil to remove toxic salts, and keeps down insects such as plant lice.

Remove fallen flowers, fading leaves, and flower stalks which have finished blooming. While this is done primarily for aesthetic reasons, it is necessary during humid, cloudy spells to prevent the flowers which have fallen on the leaves from rotting and marking the foliage. Although it is a job that must be done, it is necessary to remember that, in so doing, it is possible to transfer mites from infested plants to healthy ones. Therefore, clean up the healthy plants first and, after handling infested and suspected plants, wash hands thoroughly with soap and water before touching plants again. The flower stalks and fading leaves should be removed with a quick, sideways jerk so as to leave behind no stubs which might decay and cause trouble. To do this properly, it is necessary to have both hands free—one to steady the plant, the other to do the jerking. For convenience it is desirable to pin a paper bag to one's clothing to serve as a receptacle for the debris, which can be disposed of by putting bag and contents in a fire.

Pot Washing   This is not absolutely essential, but clean pots do help to give a collection a well-groomed appearance. With ordinary plants the usual procedure is to rest the pot (holding it with one hand) on the rim of a water-filled bucket and remove dirt with a scrub brush dipped often in the water. This method is somewhat hazardous in view of the brittle nature of saintpaulias, and probably the best way of handling the pot-washing chore is to hold the plant over a washbowl of water and wash the pot with a wet, frequently rinsed rag.

Insecticidal Spraying   Many growers are convinced of the value of regular, frequent (every two weeks) spraying with an insecticide as a prophylactic measure against mites and insect pests. My own attitude is that during winter months this might be omitted, provided no trouble develops; but during spring and summer, when pests outdoors are abundant and may enter the plant room through open windows, either under their own power or propelled by wind, it might be safer to include spraying among the bi-weekly chores. If for any reason highly poisonous sprays are out of the question, you could use those in which rotenone or pyrethrin is the principal killing agent, such as Precise Houseplant Insecticide. When there are no objections on this score, Dimite or Kelthane could be used and would be more effective against mites. Any spray that is effective against mites is likely to mar the bloom, so, unless the flowers are infested, it is advisable to apply it, so far as possible, to the foliage only.

Ventilation Many writers on the culture of African-violets insist on their need for fresh air. Ventilation is undoubtedly desirable under certain conditions; for example, when artificial gas is used for 'cooking and heating, and, when the air of the house is dry, to admit moisture-laden air from outdoors more freely. The windows of my study, where the bulk of my plants are grown, are seldom opened—in winter they are closed to keep out the cold; in summer to keep out the heat. However, this does not mean that the plants and I live in a constantly "dead" atmosphere—this is an old house far from airtight and my wife is assiduous in opening windows in her part of the establishment. And there you have the answer to the question: "Which is the best way to ventilate African-violets during cold weather?"— open the windows in an adjacent room and open the door of the plant room.

Whatever you do, don't allow a draft of cold air to blow directly on the leaves. Of course, when the outdoor temperature approximates that of the room, there is no objection to opening a window so that air blows directly on the plants, provided it is not too strong a current.

Watering has already been covered in some detail. This is just to emphasize that at some seasons and during certain weather conditions it is necessary to exercise extra care in watering. In late winter and early spring, when only a little furnace heat is needed, the relative humidity of the air increases and there is less demand by the plants for moisture at the roots. This is the season when petiole, root, and stem rots are most prevalent so it is necessary to be careful to avoid waterlogging the soil—a condition which favors their development. Again in midsummer, in those regions which suffer from high temperatures and high humidity, the soil dries out slowly, and it is better to keep the plants a little on the dry side, especially those which are not actively growing.

OUTDOORS OR INDOORS FOR SUMMER?

While house plants in general respond well to an outdoor vacation during summer, African-violets and their relative the Gloxinia usually are believed to be better off when kept indoors, or at least given the shelter provided by a porch from heavy rain and wind. However, two writers in the *African Violet Magazine*—one in Iowa, the other in California (Los Angeles)—report good results from outdoor treatment during the hot months.

The lady from Iowa, Aletha Sturdivan, put hers beneath "two huge Barberry bushes," pushing the pots into the "composty" earth for stability and to help keep the roots damp and cool. The disadvantages recorded are dirt on the foliage from splashing rains and angleworms getting into the pots—a trouble which has since, so far, been eliminated by standing the pots on ashes.

The Los Angeles lady, Clarissa Harris, puts hers in a lath house with the laths doubled to shut off the noon sun, plus "lightweight muslin" several feet below the ceiling. The plants were placed on "stepped" shelves on the benches, and protected from drafts by a glass windbreak on the windward side. Sand under the benches holds moisture and, during periods of low humidity, a spray runs for several hours under the benches but not in contact with the plants.

My own results from outdoor culture were poor to mediocre, but I must admit no particular pains were taken and the plants were left for the most part to fend for themselves. Two plants—'Viking' and 'Snow White'—were put in an open coldframe

To maintain single-crown growths, a double-crowned plant of 'Last Snow' was divided and repotted. These are the two divisions just eight weeks after being separated. Growth is symmetrical because the plants were grown under fluorescent lamps.

shaded by overhanging trees and bushes where they got no sun at all except for a short time early in the morning. These were watered occasionally when I happened to think of them and they did fairly well. The others, two or three dozen of them, were seedlings. These, except for four plants replanted in a window box, which they filled very nicely, were set out around the trunks of two enormous trees—a sugar Maple and a Buttonwood.

The soil had first been prepared by loosening it with a spading fork. After the initial sprinkle from a watering can, they had to rely on nature's supply, and although we had frequent rains well distributed throughout the summer, many of them were so meager that they failed to penetrate the canopy of foliage that shaded the saintpaulias. In order to prevent mud from splashing on the leaves, and to conserve natural moisture in the soil, each plant was "mulched" with small, flat stones. They bloomed all summer and there were still a few blooms early in October after two light frosts, which seared some of the leaves of Beans, Sweet Potatoes, and, of course, the saintpaulias.

But they never looked really happy, a fact that can easily be explained. They had been so crowded in the window box in which they had been placed (indoors), their leafstalks and roots so intermingled, that it had been impossible to remove them without a great deal of breakage from which they were slow to recover. Undoubtedly they also suffered from dryness during a great part of the summer. The four plants reset in the window box and put outside did fairly well because they were close enough to the house to get an occasional watering when needed.

I was inspired to make this trial from reading an article by B. Y. Morrison in the *National Horticultural Magazine* in which it was indicated that E. Andre, writing in *Revue Horticole,* described the use of saintpaulia planted out in a rock garden to be salvaged in the fall or left to die. It occurred to me that this might be a way of handling surplus seedlings for which there was no room in the house. I still think the idea has possibilities —but not the way I did it. The young plants must be started in pots so they can be planted outdoors without severe setback; they must be watered during dry spells; and they must be shaded completely from the midday sun.

It seems to me that each grower must decide for himself whether to keep them indoors or outdoors during the summer largely on a basis of personal convenience. They can spend the summer outdoors *provided* proper precautions are taken. These include waiting until the weather is settled and warm, when it is reasonably sure that the temperature will not fall below 60°. A concomitant is the necessity of bringing them indoors before nights become chilly in the fall. They must have a situation sheltered from high winds and be completely shaded during those hours when the sun is high. While they can endure considerable dryness at the roots, it is far better to prevent this by watering them regularly during dry spells.

If the pots are to be placed on the ground, it should first be surfaced with about 3 inches of chicken grit (or something similar) which should be thoroughly watered after it is in place to wash the dust contained in it to a lower level. This should prevent the annoyance of mud spatters as a result of heavy rain. If the pots are supported on a bench or table, it may be well to provide for constant water-level watering to reduce the time necessary for watering and to help provide atmospheric humidity. The chief hazard to be faced in many regions, however, is that of hailstorms which could ruin a collection of saintpaulias in a few minutes. It is possible to guard against this by erecting a frame with a sloping roof and providing an awning which could be rolled down whenever a storm threatens.

It seems to me that for most of us saintpaulias can be cared for with less trouble in the house or on a sheltered porch.

PRUNING: SINGLE OR MULTIPLE CROWNS?

Whether or not the plants are restricted to a single crown or allowed to develop several crowns is largely a matter of personal preference. You may occasionally get a more floriferous specimen if several crowns are allowed to develop but, on the other hand, they may become so crowded that blooming is inhibited and the beautiful rosette pattern made by the leaves is largely obscured. In general, a single-crown plant is preferred. Personally, I would restrict to a single crown all the Du Pont and similar varieties; 'Admiral', 'Commodore', and such; the Amazons and Supremes; the Girl and My Lady varieties; and those with spooned foliage. Trailers and others whose rosette of foliage is not particularly impressive and which have a tendency toward multiple crowns are sometimes allowed to grow with as many as three crowns to a pot.

Single Crown   Pruning plants to a single crown ideally should be done just as soon as the side growths are large enough to be distinguished from developing flower stalks. Probably the best way of doing this is to pinch them out with the aid of small, blunt-nosed tweezers; or they can be pushed off with the aid of a pointed nail file or a blunt-point pencil. If troubled in the not-

These photos show 'Violet Beauty' grown as a single-crown plant and as a multi-crowned clump. Some growers prefer multi-crowned plants for an abundance of flowers, but most specialists remove secondary crowns to encourage symmetry.

far-distant past with rot at the base of the petioles, it might be well to dust the wounds lightly with Fermate applied with a camel's-hair brush. When for any reason the side growths get beyond the tweezer stage, use a sharp, narrow-bladed knife to cut them off close to the main stem.

Leaf Pruning   Leaves which spoil the symmetry of single-crown plants should be snapped off as soon as it is discovered that they are out of place. Occasionally the leaves of some varieties in the Girl group grow so closely packed together that the flower stalks have difficulty in pushing their way through. In such cases the congestion should be relieved by removing one or more offending leaves. This is a ticklish job to do without injuring the leaves that are to remain and is best done piecemeal by pulling off the blade of the leaf to be removed in order to grasp the leafstalk with thumb and finger.

There are some growers who make it a practice to prune off many of the lowermost leaves, leaving only a single circle below the point of emerging flowering stalks, because they believe it enhances the appearance of the plants and promotes floriferousness. It is a matter of personal taste so far as improvement of looks is concerned, and I am doubtful whether it stimulates flower production. I believe that the removal of healthy leaves weakens the plant and that it should not be done except in the case of an occasional congested leaf or one which definitely spoils the symmetry; or when a few are required for propagational purposes; or when they are marred or abnormal.

Turning for Symmetry   When plants are illuminated from one direction only, they tend to grow toward the light and in consequence become one-sided. To avoid this, and to promote shapeliness, the pots in which they are growing should be given a quarter turn every two or three days so that all the leaves in due turn are equally exposed to light. The results are disappointing if the plant is left in one position until the leaves are visibly stretched toward the light before turning it.

Plants grown under fluorescent lamps are usually very symmetrical. Most prize-winning growers use light gardens for their show plants.

Labeling Everyone who maintains a collection of saintpaulias likes to keep track of their names. When only a few varieties are involved, it is possible to memorize them, but when a dozen or more are kept, some kind of labeling is desirable. The ordinary plastic 4-inch pot labels are adequate for leaves in process of propagation and for small potted plants, but when the crowns increase in size, the ordinary labels get in the way of developing leaves and may mar the symmetry of the plants. Furthermore, they are unsightly and stand out like sore thumbs as you may have noticed, especially in photographs of collections. An easy way to avoid this is to write the name on a piece of ½-inch adhesive about 2 inches long and stick it on the pot just below the rim. The writing can be done with waterproof ink or with a soft black pencil. Some prefer to use painters' masking tape rather than adhesive.

GROOMING PLANTS FOR EXHIBITION

There is nothing certain about this, but saintpaulias are likely to be at their best from nine to fifteen months from the time they are potted, as rooted cuttings, into their flowering-size pots. So, ordinarily, the prospective exhibitor will select and start his plants about a year ahead of the time of the exhibition.

The varieties chosen to receive special grooming, in general, should be the ones with which you are most successful. If you are "out" to grow one of the big fellows with a single crown up to 2 to 2½ feet across, your selection should include one or more of the following classics: Du Pont varieties, *S. ionantha,* 'Admiral', 'Blue Warrior', 'Norseman', 'Redhead', and 'Violet Beauty'.

Giant modern hybrids, much easier to find in catalogues, include 'Gala', 'Half and Half', 'Lavender Delight', the Rhapsodie cultivars and 'Targeteer'.

Potential Prize Winners   The kind of plant most likely to take a prize is determined in part by the kind of show at which it is to be exhibited. I once attended a flower show at a county fair at which about a dozen plants were exhibited in the class for African-violets. First and second prizes were given to two plants of 'Blue Boy'—well-grown plants of 'Du Pont Lavender Pink' and 'Lady Geneva' being completely ignored. In a show sponsored by an African-violet society, the 'Du Pont Lavender Pink' and 'Lady Geneva' would probably have been given first and second prizes because the judges would have been specialists versed in the fine points of saintpaulias. In a flower show which

'Amethyst' plant, grown for exhibition by Mrs. A. B. Bowman, has a diameter of 29 inches.

includes all kinds of plants the judges are usually general practitioners and likely to be overimpressed by a large number of flowers regardless of the nature of the variety.

Judging Points This brings us to the standards used in judging saintpaulias. The Committee on "Show Preparation and Judging" for the African Violet Society suggests the following scale of points.

Leaf pattern or form	30
(Symmetry of plant)	
Floriferousness	25
(Quantity of bloom according to variety)	
Condition	20
(Cultural perfection; freedom from diseases, insects, and marred foliage)	
Size of bloom	15
(According to variety)	
Color	10
(Color of bloom according to variety)	
Total	100

It will at once be noticed that emphasis is placed on the leaf pattern, which requires symmetry. A lopsided plant stands but little chance against one that is well-rounded. The even spacing of the leaves is another factor to be considered. This involves, in the rosette types, what the botanists call "leaf-mosaic" with the blades so disposed that there is little overlapping and no vacant spaces between them. Thus, if the lowermost leaves have excessively long petioles so that there is much space between their blades and those of the next "tier" it is counted as a demerit.

In cultural perfection the color of the leaves must be typical of the variety. They must not droop unduly because this might imply that at some time the plant was allowed to wilt because of dryness or was exposed to temperatures that are too low. Ring-spotted leaves, those marred by exposure to draft, or bleached

A perfect flower-laden rosette, measuring 23 inches across, of the variety 'My Second Prize', grown and exhibited by Mrs. Bowman.

by too much sun, those showing evidence of previous attacks by insects, all constitute defects. (Plants actually infested with insects or mites are never likely to reach the show bench; they are eliminated by the intelligence of the exhibitor, or the vigilance of the show committee anxious to protect the plants of other exhibitors.) All leaves should be well-shaped, not malformed by close contact with other leaves or with the pot label during the time they were actively increasing in size. The leaves must be clean, free from dust and debris, and exhibit the gloss and glow of perfect health.

Except in classes for non-blooming specimens, the number of blooms per plant is an important factor. In this respect the nature of the variety and age of the plant are considered. A mature plant is expected to carry more blooms than a youngster, and a discerning judge would not penalize the giant tetraploid Du Pont and Amazon varieties because their flower stalks were fewer in number than those of Ballet strain hybrids, for example. Similarly, multiple-crowned plants might be expected to carry more flowers than single-crown specimens.

The size of bloom *for the variety* also is considered. Mature flowers of the Du Pont varieties may vary from 1½ to 2½ or even 3 inches in diameter, determined by the kind of culture, age of plant and season; whereas other types may be only about 1¼ inches across. Naturally, other factors being equal, the plant with the largest blooms in each class gets the prize.

The color of the blooms is a variable factor, affected by soil, exposure, and season. Some typically pale gray-blue, nearly white, blooms may sometimes deepen in color to approach the flowers of *ionantha;* while another plant's flowers, ordinarily white, may become flushed with pink. The judges who know their business will give the greatest number of points for color to the flowers which most nearly approach the accepted color for the variety.

Great size is not necessarily desirable although a good big plant will usually score over a good small one.

Start Right In order to produce plants which will be in the running against severe competition, it is necessary to be meticulous in everything pertaining to good culture. Start with healthy young plants in good soil. When they are thoroughly established and the roots permeate the soil, give supplementary feedings every ten days or two weeks with liquid fertilizer, either wholly of animal origin or alternating with those of inorganic (chemical) origin.

Keep the soil constantly moist and provide the optimum in light, humidity, and temperature. Give the plants a preferred position and do not crowd them. Turn the pot frequently to insure even, all-round illumination. Train them in the way they should go—if one or two leaves project far beyond the remainder, remove them. If developing leaves are not proceeding in quite the right direction, it may be possible to steer them by pushing into the soil a slender stick alongside the leafstalk to exert a gentle pressure toward the right direction. (Remember the brittle nature of saintpaulia and do this with great care.)

Giant 'Targeteer' has double deep purple-blue flowers, scalloped foliage, and prominent yellow anthers. A ring at left helps judge the size of 'Targeteer' blooms.

If through inadvertence the plant becomes chilled or the soil is allowed to become too dry so that the outer leaves droop abnormally over the side of the pot, it may be possible to correct the condition by supporting the leaves at the right angle. To do this, allow the soil to become dry enough to reduce the brittleness of the leafstalks, then set the plant in a bowl deep enough and wide enough to allow the outer leaf blades to rest on its edge in their normal position. Then water the plant and wait a few days until the stalks become stiffened. Another way is to put crumpled newspaper in a shallow carton, make a nest in the middle, and set the plant in it so that the leaves are held up by the surrounding paper.

Be assiduous in removing unwanted side growths before they become large enough to interfere with the symmetrical development of the main crown. Even plants destined for entry in the multiple-crown class can sometimes be improved by pruning out, six weeks or more before show time, superfluous weak crowns which have no chance of reaching the blooming stage in time. Don't take out any crowns that would leave an unsightly gap, and be careful in removing any of them because one or more leaves may be entangled with some which could ill be spared and which a hasty tug might break off.

Transportation Tips After spending a year or more in growing a first-class plant, naturally you will want it to arrive intact at the place of exhibition. Remember that saintpaulias are just about the most difficult plants of all to transport without breakage and you will understand why any neglect of precautions to insure their safety is unwise. In any plant of show caliber the spread of the leaves usually is greatly in excess of the diameter of the pot, and in most varieties it is unsafe to draw the leaves together so that the plants can be bundled to occupy less space. Therefore, the plants must be packed with their leaves spread out naturally, which involves containers of considerable area.

For journeys of one hundred miles or so by automobile over good roads I have found the following method suffices for large plants. Use a strong carton a foot or so high, equal in its smallest horizontal dimension to the spread of the plant. Place an empty pot of the same size as that of the plant in the carton and pack crumpled newspaper solidly around it to hold it firmly in place. To provide proper support, the slope of the surface of the newspaper must conform to the position taken by the lowermost leaves—if they droop downward, the newspaper should slope down from the rim; if the angle is upward, then the paper should slope up to correspond. The objective is to provide a soft bed on which the leaves can rest. Having prepared the nest, remove the empty pot (or leave it in place) and slip in the plant. Some plants have such a dense crown of leaves that it is practically impossible to lift them from above so it is necessary to put a hand beneath the crown to grasp the pot. In order to transfer it safely, it is advisable to slit two corners of the carton so that a side or end can be folded down to permit easy insertion; then the flap is turned up and tied in place.

If more than one plant is to be transported, preliminary cogitation and measurement may make it possible to get several plants in one package. For example: if you have one 18-inch plant and four smaller ones, and the carton is 18×24 inches, it might be possible to put the big fellow in the center with a small one in each of the four corners; or you might be able to squeeze in six or seven medium-size plants. If the road to be traveled is a rough one and the journey long, it would be desirable to anchor the pots and roots to prevent them from being jounced out of their nests. To do this, wad moss or moist newspaper between the surface of the soil and the leaf bases. Then cut wood cleats to fit the width of the inside of the carton, press them firmly on the pot rim two to each plant, and fasten in place with thumbtacks pushed through the carton from outside. The cleats can be something of the nature of builders' wooden laths wrapped in paper to present a smooth surface which will not abrade the leaves.

SOCIETIES

The AFRICAN VIOLET SOCIETY OF AMERICA was founded in 1946 by a group of enthusiastic hobbyists and several commercial growers. Since that time thousands of members have joined the group and official A.V.S.A. shows have been sponsored throughout the United States. The society welcomes everyone to membership.

Many members who never attend the shows still enjoy their membership for the opportunity it gives them to correspond with fellow enthusiasts and to receive the colorful *African Violet Magazine* five times each year. The society now has about 25,000 members, some of whom are residents in other countries. For a free culture folder and information about membership, write to: The African Violet Society of America; P.O. Box 1326; Knoxville, Tennessee 37901.

In addition to membership activity, the society is also the official International Registration Authority for the genus *Saintpaulia*. See Chapter 11 for hybrid registration information. The society receives registrations from around the world, publishes them in the magazine, and from time to time issues a Master Variety List which includes registration information from several previous years.

Several other societies include saintpaulias in their area of interest, although their publications do not specialize in African-violets exclusively. The GESNERIAD SOCIETY INTERNATIONAL and SAINTPAULIA INTERNATIONAL share a publication called the *Gesneriad Saintpaulia News*. This color-illustrated magazine, published every other month, is sent to members who pay full dues to either society. For information, write to: Saintpaulia International; P.O. Box 549; Knoxville, Tennessee 37901.

The AMERICAN GLOXINIA AND GESNERIAD SOCIETY is a group that includes saintpaulia within the broad interest group of all gesneriads. If you are interested in growing companion gesneriads with your African-violets, the bimonthly *Gloxinian* magazine should be of interest. For membership information, write to: Mrs. Charlotte M. Rowe, Membership Secretary; American Gloxinia and Gesneriad Society; P.O. Box 174; New Milford, Connecticut 06776.

If you grow plants under lights, you will enjoy membership in the INDOOR LIGHT GARDENING SOCIETY OF AMERICA. Their bimonthly magazine includes cultural information for gesneriads. For information write to: The Indoor Light Gardening Society of America; 128 West 58th Street; New York, New York 10019.

CHAPTER 9

Adding to your Collection

Beginners used to start off with 'Blue Boy', 'White Lady', and 'Pink Beauty', all good varieties, and once popular with many of the large commercial growers. Now the adaptable Ballet and Rhapsodie hybrids, carried by chain stores and many growers nationwide, are the first African-violets most often selected by beginners.

When you wish to add to your collection, it is just as well first to see what the local florist and department stores have to offer. But buy with discrimination; don't take a plant merely because it is a little different from those you have. It should have some other endearing qualities and it should be labeled with its variety name, otherwise you may be buying the same thing by mail later on thinking you are getting something new.

Look at the plants carefully to try to determine if they are suffering from any malady. Pay particular attention to the central part of the crown, having first made yourself familiar with the symptoms of mite infestation as described in Chapter 7. I have seen plants offered for sale so infested with mites that, if they were able to organize, would have no difficulty in walking the plant out of the store. Beware of damaged plants offered at a reduced price. If it is just a case of mechanical injury they may be a bargain, but if their ratty appearance is caused by mites, insects, or disease, the acquisition might be unprofitable even if you were paid to take them.

Lyndon Lyon's growing range and Fischer Greenhouses are typical of modern commercial firms which offer hundreds of different hybrids. Visitors are welcome at both nurseries.

After exhausting strictly local possibilities, make inquiry (of your florist among others) to discover if there is a specialist in African-violets operating within easy driving distance and pay him a visit. It may be rewarding in more ways than one. If he is a good grower it will be possible to see how it should be done; you will be able, perhaps, to get hints on culture and advice on how to overcome your troubles, if any; and you may find there a source of potting soil and pest destroyers as well as varieties new to your collection.

Seek Good Supplies   But if you are a rabid collector, this will not suffice. No one dealer grows *all* the varieties of saintpaulia available and of those that are carried in the establishment you visit, not all will appeal to you. So another source must be sought which can be found in mail-order firms. There are many of these scattered all over the United States, and you can learn their addresses in various ways. By this time you are probably a member of a local African-violet club, and/or of the African Violet Society of America, and can inquire of your fellow members and consult the advertisements in the *African Violet Magazine* (the official organ of the Society) and write to growers for their lists and catalogues.

When comparing prices of dealers, remember that they vary for different varieties—the older ones and those which propagate readily are naturally less expensive than those which are in short supply. Then notice the grade of plants offered: whether in flower or not, and the size of pot from which they are shipped—a plant from a 2- or 2¼-inch pot should cost less than one from a 3- or 4-inch size. Some dealers sell leaves for propagational purposes (some sell nothing but leaves), and these afford an inexpensive way of adding to your collection if you are willing to wait a few months for blooms. Then, having surveyed the situation, make up a list of the varieties you want and select from it a few with the idea of sending a small trial order to each of the firms which seem most promising. This is for the purpose of getting a line on the quality of the plants supplied by various firms and whether or not their packing methods are adequate. If possible, place your order during the summer or spring. Saintpaulias are sensitive to cold and most growers refuse to ship, or are reluctant to do so, during the coldest months.

Packing Is Important In the early days of shipping saintpaulias, packages sent by parcel post or express often arrived in deplorable condition—sometimes frozen and sometimes with most of the leaves broken off. Nowadays most mail-order dealers have solved the problem of proper packing, and I have received plants in almost perfect condition on arrival from Pennsylvania, Massachusetts, Indiana, Michigan, Georgia, and Arkansas. Strangely enough, the only plants which arrived badly battered were from comparatively nearby New Jersey; and the shipment which arrived in the best condition had the longest trip of all— from far-away Arkansas. This last consisted of a single plant in a 2¼-inch clay pot. The soil was held in place by a wad of waxed paper stuffed between the leaves and the soil surface. The pot was wrapped in moist sphagnum moss covered with waxed paper and tied in place. The plant was then laid in the center of a piece of corrugated cardboard, to which it was fastened in two places with cellulose tape to prevent sliding. The cardboard was then rolled into a cylinder around the plant, taped again, and wrapped in newspaper. The package was then placed in the middle of a carton 7½ × 7½ × 14 inches, with crumpled newspaper packed all around it to prevent shifting and to minimize temperature changes encountered en route.

Another package, this one from Massachusetts (packed in much the same way except that moss was used to hold the soil in the pot and it was taped in place before wrapping in waxed paper), also arrived in good condition but with one leaf broken. This was understandable, seeing that, of the six plants in the package, two were Du Pont varieties, notoriously difficult to pack and ship successfully because of their excessively brittle leafstalks which sometimes spread horizontally from the crown.

When packing a small plant for shipment, surround the pot with moss extending a little above the crown and hold in place with several rubber bands or thin twine.

The next step in packing is to wrap the plant in waxed paper and secure it to corrugated cardboard with strips of adhesive across the pot. Finally, roll, tape, and label the package.

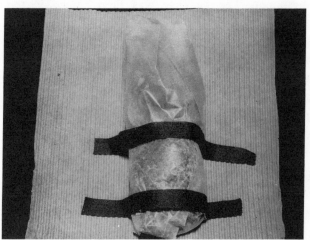

I have gone into some detail regarding packing methods for two reasons: one, in case you should want to mail a plant; two, to indicate that a safe system of packing is obviously expensive and accounts for the difference in the price of plants picked up from a greenhouse and those sent by mail or express.

There are variants in packing methods, of course. Most growers, to reduce shipping charges, remove the plants from clay pots and transfer them to paper pots or wrap the soil balls in moss. This works all right in most cases, but not when the plant has been growing for too short a time in the pot so that the soil is not fully permeated with roots to hold the ball together. There are some who substitute cotton for moss in packing. This is just as effective as moss, but irritating to the recipient because of the time he has to spend in picking "fluffies" from the plants.

How to Unpack Plants   Carefully packed plants suggests equal care in unpacking. The carton should be opened at once and the plants laid out on a bench or table. If they have been frozen or are badly battered, notify the post office or express company and the sender. Take your time in removing the mummylike wrappings—an impatient yank may separate crown from roots. So use scissors or a sharp knife to cut tapes or strings, and watch out to avoid missing the label carrying the varietal name so that it is not inadvertently placed in the wastepaper basket with the wrappings. As each plant is unwrapped, lay it on the table with the root ball covered with damp moss, and broken-off leaves, if any, alongside. When all are laid out, you can decide to better advantage what is needed in the way of pots, labels, et cetera.

Except for plants in 3- or 4-inch pots, repotting is almost certain to be necessary. Multiple-crown plants should be examined to decide whether they are ready to be divided (see Chapter 11) or whether it would be better to pot them up "as is" and wait awhile before performing the operation. Well-rooted single-crown plants from 2- to 2½-inch pots can be shifted into 3½- to 4½-inch size (according to their apparent vigor), in which they can stay for a year or so.

African violets sold by mail-order specialists usually come in 2½-inch plastic pots. Let them adjust to your conditions for a month or so before moving them on to slightly larger pots.

The name of the variety may be written on the outside of the package, on a slip of paper in among the leaves of the plant, or on a plastic pot label stuck in the soil. Permanent labels may be of small strips of adhesive or masking tape stuck on the new pots. The wooden pot labels will suffice for a while; or you may need them to label the broken leaves which, of course, you will put in the propagating case or flat, giving you an excuse to make a permanent label for the parent plant. Plastic labels last almost indefinitely.

When potting is completed, the plants should be thoroughly watered with an overhead spray of tepid water to serve the double purpose of moistening the soil and of washing any debris or crumbs of soil from the leaves.

If you are *very* fearful of receiving mites with these new acquisitions, you should wear an apron which can be taken off and dropped in a pan of very hot water as soon as the job is done. Then take the plants to their living quarters isolated from the rest of the collection, shade with newspaper laid over them until the leaves are dry if the situation is at any time sunny, and thoroughly wash your hands with hot, soapy water before handling any other plants. They should remain in the isolation ward for 2 to 2½ months. If no trouble has developed in this time, you can be reasonably sure that they are clean.

Don't be surprised if plants in bloom when received shed their corollas, become sulky, and stop blooming. Saintpaulias are temperamental, and a sudden change in environment, coupled with the jolts, jouncings, and close confinement while on the journey, may so shock them that they temporarily refuse to blossom. Give them a chance and they will usually snap out of it.

Swapping Leaves I've left until last the cheapest way of adding to an African-violet collection, and that is by exchange of leaves with other amateurs—either personal friends, or acquaintances secured through club contacts; or by mediums of exchange called "Homing Pigeons" or other ornithological names, promoted by certain plant magazines. Doubtless this is great fun and you may make interesting contacts in addition to augmenting your collection. Perhaps your chances of getting a dose of mites are a little greater than if you rely on commercial growers who cannot afford to send out infested plants; and perhaps occasionally you may get a wrongly named plant—which may also happen in a commercial shipment. I would not be deterred by either of those possibilities; the chances are that nothing disastrous will happen—not if you are on the alert to nip trouble in the bud.

One advantage: there is no difficulty about packing and shipping leaves for propagational purposes. Merely wrap each leaf, with its name on a slip of paper, in a piece of waxed paper and fasten the edges of the paper with pins or staples. Put the leaves loosely in a small cardboard box (heavy enough to go through the mails without crushing) with enough crumpled tissue paper to keep them from sliding around. Wrap, address, and mail first-class or special delivery if you want them to get to their destination quickly. If they have a long way to go it might be well to put a little wad of moist moss or cotton, held in place by metal foil or waxed paper, on the base of the stalk before wrapping the whole in waxed paper.

PATENTED PLANTS

By an amendment to the patent laws by Congress in 1930 it was established that the originator or discoverer of a plant (exclusive of those propagated by seeds and tubers) distinct from any previously known species or variety could, after compliance with certain rules, patent it and secure the control of its asexual (vegetative, by cuttings, division, et cetera) propagation and distribution for a period of seventeen years.

Many new varieties of saintpaulia have been patented, and this fact is made known to the purchaser by a statement on the tag or label which bears the name of the variety and which should accompany the plant or propagating material wherever it is sold or given away. Such plants may not be propagated asexually without the permission of the owner of the patent—not even for your own use, or to give away. Therefore, if you have obtained any patented varieties of African-violets and wish to propagate them in any way except by seeds, and are law-abiding, it will be necessary to obtain written permission to propagate from the owner of the patent. He will supply the labels, with variety name and statement that it is patented, one of which must be affixed to every plant propagated and to every leaf sold or given away for propagational purposes. The agreements between the holder of a patent and those seeking the right to propagate the patented plant vary according to circumstances—the patentee may place a limit on the number of plants which may be propagated and otherwise restrict their distribution. Usually a charge of $6.00 per 100 labels is made, which represents the royalty accruing to the holder of the patent.

The best-known patented hybrids are Ballet and Rhapsodie selections. The series most recently released under full patent protection are called Optimara hybrids. The Optimaras are named after the various United States of America.

CHAPTER 10

Greenhouse Culture

Although perfectly good plants of saintpaulia can be grown in an ordinary dwelling, sometimes lack of room to grow as many plants as are wanted makes a greenhouse eminently desirable. Furthermore, because the illumination is more uniform, it is easy to grow symmetrical plants without the twisting and turning that are necessary when the light comes from one side. Also one can splash water around on evaporating surfaces to promote the necessary humidity with a mind free from worry because there are no furnishings or parquet floors to be harmed by it.

Location Ordinarily small greenhouses are attached to the dwelling and in some cases may be an extension of one of the rooms. Because saintpaulias can get along in relatively dim light, it is not necessary to set the greenhouse on the south side of the dwelling. Even the north side could be used and would help solve the shading problem in summer, but one has to take into consideration the cost of heating which is greater if on the north (on the west also); and, in regions with many sunless days in winter, the amount of light might be less than the optimum. In general I would say that the east side is preferable.

Heating Enough radiation (or hot-air ducts of sufficient capacity) should be provided to maintain a minimum of 60° (better, 65°) on the coldest nights to be expected in the locality. The

A modern lean-to greenhouse is easy to erect and lasts for many years. Automatic controls make ventilation, heating, and humidification an easy matter.

temperature can be allowed to rise ten to fifteen degrees during the day.

The kind of heating system used is determined largely by local circumstances. When the greenhouse is small (less than 100 square feet) and is attached to the house over a cellar window, air from near the cellar ceiling can be blown into the greenhouse by a circulating fan controlled by a thermostat located in the greenhouse, and may suffice most of the time if the cellar is a hot one. During certain weather conditions it may be necessary to help out by putting a wick-type kerosene heater in the greenhouse; or, if electricity is not too expensive, a thermostatically controlled electric heating unit could be used. In those favored regions where electricity can be had for almost nothing, the heating could be entirely by this means.

If the greenhouse is attached, or near, to a dwelling heated by steam or hot water, and if the boiler has enough capacity, it should be relatively easy to run a hot-water main from the boiler to the greenhouse, distributing the heat by regular heater pipes or by fin convectors. The temperature is controlled by a thermostat in the greenhouse which operates a small electric motor circulator when heat is called for.

When the home is heated by hot air, an additional duct can be connected to the system and run out to the greenhouse, with a return duct provided to draw off cool air from the floor. A thermostat controls the blower which pushes hot air into the greenhouse. This system should not be used if there is any possibility of coal gas, or artificial gas, finding its way into the cellar or room in which the heater is installed, and from which air is drawn, because both are extremely toxic to plants. In most cases it is desirable to supplement the hot air by an electric heater, because heat is lost more quickly from a greenhouse with its extensive glass area than it is in a home, and the greenhouse thermostat may be calling for heat before the one in the home indicates a need for it.

For free-standing greenhouses of 150 square feet or more, self-contained, oil-burning, hot-water circulating units are available. Boilers heated by coal or artificial gas can be used in such situations provided they are contained in separate compartments to eliminate the danger of lethal gas finding its way into the greenhouse. Such systems usually make use of hot water circulating by gravity, which requires the installation of the boiler at a lower level than the greenhouse.

Other fuels which may be used include natural gas, bottled gas, and distilled oil (not catalytic process oil) burned in a "pot-type" oil burner.

Before deciding on a heating system, discuss the matter with a heating engineer, and get as much information as possible from firms specializing in greenhouse construction.

Furnishings The greenhouse needs a number of furnishings. These include benches on which to stand the plants, plumbing and piping to carry water, and possibly a cistern in which water can be tempered prior to use, a portable potting table unless a workroom is attached to the greenhouse, and, possibly, a propagating area.

Benches usually are made of concrete or wood, though they may be all steel, or steel frame with pipe legs and slate flooring.

Concrete has the advantages and disadvantages of permanence. Wood benches are cheaper to install and are easier to change if you find on use that the layout is not ideal. They are fairly long-lasting if cypress or redwood is used, or if less durable woods are treated with copper naphthanate (Cuprinol) to delay decay. *Do not use creosote* as a preservative on any of the wooden members of a greenhouse—its fumes are toxic to plants.

It pays to give considerable thought to the layout and to the type of bench to be installed. Among the things to be considered are width of benches, height from floor, width of walks, and the proposed method of watering.

The width of the bench should not exceed 3 feet, and for most persons (especially those of low stature with short arms) 2½ feet is preferable in view of the nature of the plant material which requires close attention and careful handling. If 3-foot benches are used and overhead watering is contemplated, the desirability of installing wooden "stages" of two steps on the bench to provide three levels is worth serious thought. By so doing the plants can be displayed to better advantage and it is easier to get at them for overhead watering and other ministrations. If the house is wide enough to permit a central bench, this can be (if there is room) twice the width of the side benches, because it can be reached from two sides.

There are four things to be considered in determining the height of the bench: the height of the person who is most concerned with the care of the plants, whether or not the plants are to be arranged on stages, whether or not the plants are to be grown in double bunks, and the amount of headroom in the house.

Thirty inches is the usual bench height, but for those who are 6 feet or over, the addition of 6 inches to this is desirable if practicable. The lowermost level should not be in excess of 30 inches if some of the plants are to be displayed on stages, because the two steps (shelves) with 4- or 5-inch risers would bring the plants on the top shelf out of convenient reach. If the double-bunk system is used, the topmost bench should be 4 feet from

Thousands of African-violets live on this revolving Ferris-wheel bench at Buell's Greenhouses in Eastford, Connecticut. The wheel turns around all day to give each shelf equal light.

the ground with the lower one midway between it and the floor. The walk should be as wide as possible, consistent with not too much space wasting, to permit light to reach the plants in the lower bunks. (Commercial growers who are cramped for space sometimes use this system—growing the newly potted rooted cuttings on the lowermost bench and moving them upstairs to initiate flower bud formation.) It is a moot point as to whether it is desirable for amateurs because it results in the display plants being held at too high a level to be viewed at their best. Personally, if pushed for space, I would be inclined to string along with a compromise—using a 3-foot bench with a narrow shelf (8 inches) supported on brackets 18 inches below. Saintpaulia addicts are fortunate in dealing with plants which do not require a great deal of headroom, and so long as there is from 12 to 18 inches between the bench (or the top step of the stage) and the eaves, all will be well.

Walks should be at least 2 feet wide for comfort in navigating them—personally, being of rather large proportions, I would prefer 2½ or even 3 feet. Usually, however, the width of the walk is arrived at by a series of compromises, taking into consideration the width of the house and the benches. Usually the walks are made of concrete which can be colored, if desired, for aesthetic reasons. Brick walks laid on a cement base and pointed up with mortar are practical and good-looking. Avoid gravel, sand, cinders, and anything else which can creep into open-toed shoes or be tracked into the house. Duckboards also are taboo because they are hazardous to wearers of high-heeled shoes.

The spaces beneath the benches offer great temptations to those untidy spirits who welcome any place in which things can be thrown to be more or less out of sight; and to the plantsman who sees opportunity for growing this and that—at least along the walk edges. But it is better, on the whole, to keep the under-bench space rigorously clean and surfaced with sand or stone chips. If used to store dirty pots, the appearance of the house is marred; if plants are grown there, they may be neglected (usually they are in such situations) and become a focal point of infestation from which thrips or mites or mealybugs may be spread to the plants above.

Space under the benches can be utilized to grow plants if you install fluorescent lamps. Watering and grooming saintpaulias under the benches requires agility, but by using artificial light you can fully utilize all this warm humid space.

The method of watering to be followed determines the structure of the benches. If constant water-level watering (see below) is to be practiced, the bench must be perfectly level, watertight, and have sides about 4 inches high. For overhead watering, the bench needs to be only tight enough to hold the gravel, sand, or stone chips on which the pots are stood, and if the sides are 1 inch high it will be enough to hold the gravel, et cetera, in place.

Overhead Watering   The kind of water piping also is contingent upon the method of watering adopted. When the watering is from overhead, some system of warming the water to the air temperature of the house, or a little higher, must be adopted. This can be a cistern of sufficient capacity for one watering, situated in a warm spot near the ridge from which water is conducted by gravity to the plants by a lightweight hose fitted with a "pistol-grip" shutoff valve. After each watering the cistern is refilled so that it becomes warm enough to use for the next watering. If you prefer to apply the water with a battery filler or the watering-can method, a cistern can be installed near the hottest part of the heating system from which water can be dipped as needed. This, too, should be refilled after each watering. If it cannot conveniently be placed in a warm spot, set it where it *is* convenient and rely on a kettle of hot water to raise the temperature to the required degree.

I suspect, however, that the best and most time-saving method of solving the greenhouse watering problem (assuming that hot and cold water under pressure are available) is to make use of a thermostatic mixing valve so that water of the right temperature can be delivered to the plants.

Whether to use the common commercial method of applying the water through a sprinkler head attached to the hose, or directly to the soil by means of a low-pressure (open the faucet only part way) solid stream, depends partly on the amount of time that can be allotted to watering (the sprinkler method is faster) and partly on whether the water temperature can be relied on to be a few degrees above the air temperature. I would suggest trying the sprinkler method first and if ring-spot or other foliage injury develops, switch to the method which avoids wetting the leaves.

Constant Water-level Watering   The principle of this method already has been described in Chapter 6. Some modifications, however, are necessary under greenhouse conditions because of the larger areas involved. The bench should be level, watertight, and 4 to 6 inches deep. Lengths of a steel angle with the points of the "V" down are placed on the bottom of the bench, extending the full length, to conduct water. A partition is set off at one end large enough to contain a float valve to control the water level. In this partition there should be a drainage hole with stopper so that water can be lowered or drained off completely if this should at any time be necessary. About 2 inches of turkey grits, road chips, or similar easily permeable material is put in the bottom and surfaced with 2 to 3 inches of sand carefully leveled. The pots (ordinary porous clay pots) are pressed ¼ inch into the sand and the float adjusted to maintain the water level about 1 inch below the base of the pots. Because the pots, and the soil in them, vary in their ability to take up water by capillarity, it is necessary to keep a close watch on the bench, especially during the first few weeks, to make any necessary adjustments—those which are not getting enough water should be pressed deeper into the sand, those which are getting too much should be raised somewhat. Initially, the sand should be flooded to insure that it is in close contact with the pot. Under some conditions of weather it may be necessary to spot-water individual plants from overhead. The plants are potted in the usual way (in regular porous clay pots) except that only one piece of broken pot is put over the drainage hole to keep the soil from sifting through.

For fuller details, working drawings, et cetera, get in touch with your State Agricultural Experiment Station; or consult *Florist Crop Production and Marketing* by Kenneth Post, which you probably can get through your local public library.

Which Watering Method to Use?   Surface watering permits one more readily to shift the plants to accommodate variance in rate

These African-violets at Lyndon Lyon's greenhouse are on capillary mats under cool white/warm white fluorescent lamps.

of growth and to display them to best advantage. It is preferable when a large number of varieties of different habit are grown and when there is much difference in pot size. The chore of watering, however, is more time-consuming than the constant water-level system which has definite advantages when one's time is limited or when the plants may have to be left unattended for several days. (This last is permissible only when the house is automatically heated and ventilated and when the system has been in operation long enough to iron out quirks.) Under favorable conditions the soil is kept more uniformly moist so that the plants grow better. It is well adapted for varieties of uniform growth in pots of similar size. In spite of these advantages I feel that most amateurs who grow saintpaulias solely for pleasure will prefer surface watering.

POTTING BENCH AND SOIL CONTAINERS

An adjacent workroom is a great convenience, permitting the greenhouse to be used exclusively for the growth and display of the plants. Often this is not possible, however, and provision must be made so that soil can be stored until used and potting can be done without disrupting the household.

Soil for potting (after it has been "sterilized") can be placed in clean, covered garbage cans and kept in a garage or outdoors, bringing it into the greenhouse a day or so prior to the time of using so that it will thaw out if frozen and warm up to house temperature. The dry peat-lite mixes sold commercially (Pro, Jiffy, Terra-Lite, et cetera) thaw quickly. Small quantities reach room temperature in about six hours. Soil could be kept all the time in the greenhouse, under the benches, but, as you know, I have a feeling that this space should be kept free of extraneous matter.

A portable potting table provides the answer when there is no regular workroom. This should be about 3 feet long (or long enough to straddle the walk) and about 2 feet wide. It should have a back and two ends about 9 inches high to help keep the soil from spilling where it is not wanted, leaving the front open for convenience in working. It can be made of waterproof plywood suitably reinforced, or of tongue-and-groove flooring with ¾-inch boards forming the sides and back.

When in use, enough plants are moved to make room, as it straddles the walk and rests on the edges of two benches. If additional height is needed for convenience of working, maybe a brick laid flat beneath each corner will be enough to accomplish this; if not, make a frame of wood 2×2 inches with legs long enough to bring the table to the required height.

If the table is used when turning plants from their pots to determine if they are infested with nematodes or root rots, always cover it with several thicknesses of newspaper to avoid the danger of contaminating the worktable. Then, if pests are discovered, the plants, soil, pots, and everything can be gathered in the paper, taken to the incinerator, and burned.

When potting is in progress, always have a receptacle nearby in which discarded soil, plant debris, et cetera, can be dumped for easy removal. This, of course, is in the interests of tidiness and sanitation.

PROPAGATING SPACE

The air of a greenhouse ordinarily is damp enough to prevent the wilting of cuttings of saintpaulia so that no special precautions need be taken to insure humid conditions about them. Therefore, in most cases a good-looking shallow box of suitable area containing 2 or 3 inches of rooting medium is all that is required. If the box is 6 or 8 inches deep, the sides will help shade the cuttings and minimize stray air currents. In very dry circumstances, a pane of glass cut to fit the box, to form a "roof," could be used to contain the humid air rising from the moist rooting medium. Such a box could also be used to contain seeds sown in individual small pots or seed pans.

The space reserved for propagating should be in that portion of the house which gets least light and, preferably, where there is the greatest concentration of heat below the bench—it is desirable in propagating to have the rooting medium a few degrees higher than the air temperature to stimulate root formation.

When the plants are watered by the constant water-level method, the entire bench space, except where the pots are actually standing, can be used for cuttings, choosing first those areas where there is most shade and the sand is warmest. If seeds are to be sown, a space should be cleared to contain a box like that described two paragraphs previous to this.

SHADING

Diminishing the intensity of the sunlight is an important factor in the successful greenhouse cultivation of saintpaulias. The amount of shade provided should vary with the seasons and in accord with the aspect of the house (naturally less will be needed if the greenhouse is shaded by the dwelling) and the light intensity normally experienced in the region. The ideal to aim at is between 900 and 1,100 foot-candles for flowering plants (2,000 foot-candles is permissible for short periods). You can get by with about 500 foot-candles for starting of young plants. If you have a photographic light-exposure meter with suitable masks (or can borrow one) so that the incident light can be measured directly in foot-candles on the dial, it would be worthwhile to use it from time to time as a guide. However, the chief reliance should be placed on the behavior of the plants. (See Chapter 2, Aspect.)

In most regions, even in winter, some shade is needed to prevent the possibility of foliage injury. This can be provided permanently by painting the inside of the glass with a thin coat of cold-water (or oil), white paint, or by putting a heavy coat of whitewash on the outside of the glass in the spring which may be expected to wash off gradually as a result of summer rains so that by fall it is thin enough to admit an adequate amount of winter sunlight. If enough does not wash off naturally, scrubbing with a dry, stiff bristle brush will do the trick.

I've had no experience in growing saintpaulias under frosted glass (except for some 'Blue Boys' in a large greenhouse where they did well planted in a rock wall which shaded them from the west) but have had satisfactory results with a general collection of tropical plants. Maybe it would answer as the permanent shade for saintpaulias though I suspect supplementary shading would be necessary during the summer. Perhaps someone who likes to experiment and has some money to spend would like to try it and report on the results.

Removable Shades Ideally, part of the shading should be removable so that more light can be admitted on cloudy days. This may be of wooden slats fastened together with metal and equipped with cords so that they can easily be rolled up (these are obtainable from concerns specializing in greenhouse building); or interior shades of white cloth with metal rings sewed a foot apart in rows 2 feet apart. These slide on tightly stretched wires, spaced 2 feet apart, extending from the eaves to a bar running the length of the house a sufficient distance below the ridge so as not to interfere with the equipment controlling ventilation.

'Gypsy Trail', a trailing hybrid.

'Jennifer', a vigorous standard hybrid with an unusual color combination and fine hairs all over the bold flowers.

'Last Snow' is subject to mutations and flower color changes due to culture. The pink color of one plant's flowers is evidence of this.

'Lora Lou', a semiminiature trailer with variegated foliage.

'Happy Trails', a modern trailing hybrid.

'Wee Lass', a miniature hybrid with long-lasting one-inch flowers
on tiny four- to five-inch plants.

'Tipt', a hybrid with bold color contrast.

'Pixie Blue', an outstanding semiminiature trailer.

These have the additional advantage of preventing cold air currents from blowing directly on the plants when the ventilators are open. They are operated by cords running from the bottom hem, which envelops a metal or wooden rod, to pulleys on the bar near the ridge. I don't know of any commercial source for this kind so I'm afraid if you use them they will have to be "homemade."

Shading Paint This has to be determined largely by the individual. Personally, I would paint the inside of the glass lightly with cold-water paint (if the house is free of plants so that there is no danger of spattering the leaves) supplemented by wooden slat shades on the outside which can be rolled up or down according to the weather. The shading on the movable sash forming the ventilators has to be semi-permanent—being applied in the spring and removed in the fall. It can be sections of slat shades cut to fit or a heavy coat of whitewash.

Here are some formulas for whitewash which can be applied to the outside of the glass by spraying or, better, by a broad brush.

1. Whiting mixed to the right consistency with gasoline. Better not smoke when using this, nor make up too much at a time.

2. The following formula is recommended by the Missouri Botanical Garden:
   Water   3 gallons
   Whiting   5 pounds
   Cement   6 pounds
   Powdered glue   ½ pound
   Dissolve glue in hot water and add to mixture just before applying it to the glass. It wears off gradually.

3. Some commercial saintpaulia growers recommend the addition of 1 quart of heated linseed oil to 2 gallons of mixed whiting. (About 4 pounds of whiting to 1 gallon.)

4. You can save yourself trouble in measuring and weighing by buying ready-to-mix greenhouse shading from dealers in garden supplies.

VENTILATION

Ventilation can be provided by manually operated ventilators or automatically by an electric motor controlled by a thermostat. Preferably, ventilators should extend on both sides of the entire length of the ridge so that in windy weather the one on the leeward side can be opened while that to the windward is kept closed to avoid cold air blowing directly on the plants. When two lines of ventilators are installed, manual operation is necessary because, so far as I know, there is no automatic gadget available which takes into account the direction of the wind. In most prefabricated greenhouses, where ridge ventilators are supplied on one side only, they are made to open on the side opposite to the direction of the prevailing cold winds. In regions where the summers are hot, ventilators in both side walls beneath the benches are desirable.

The primary purpose of ventilators is to control, so far as possible, temperature and humidity. Ordinarily they are closed whenever the outside temperature falls below 60°, but during cold, muggy weather, in spring and fall, it is desirable to open them an inch or so (even though it requires extra fire heat to maintain the temperature) to insure circulation of the air and to reduce excessive humidity.

During the warm months all the ventilators should be fully open throughout the day, except if it is very windy, when those on the windward side must be closed. At night the top ventilators should be left partly open, except when the outdoor temperature is expected to drop below 65°.

Even if someone is around all the time to attend to ventilation, the automatic kind is desirable if only to take charge during those hours of sunshine before getting-up time in the morning and during the occasional mental lapses of the operator. But even when an automatic system is installed, and is working the best it can according to its lights, it is necessary sometimes for someone with brains to take a hand in the case of unusual weather conditions, such as those mentioned in the preceding paragraph, of which the machine is unaware and therefore ignores.

In general, it may be said that the objective during the cold months is control ventilation so as to maintain a minimum of 65° with a rise of 10° to 15° from sun heat during the day; and during the warm months to prevent the temperature, so far as it can be done by shading and ventilation, from rising above 80°. Ventilators should be opened every day, if only by a crack, except in bitterly cold weather, when it is difficult to maintain the temperature without using excessive fire heat, and when strong winds are blowing plenty of fresh air through the cracks and between the glass laps.

HUMIDITY

Because there are more plants all transpiring moisture from their leaves, and more evaporating surfaces—floors, benches, and walks—which can be doused with water, it is easier to maintain the desired relative humidity of about 75 per cent in a greenhouse than it is in a dwelling. The amount of "damping down" of walks and benches necessary to provide sufficient air moisture is determined by the humidity outdoors and the amount of artificial heat in the greenhouse. During sunny, cold days in winter, it may be desirable to wet down the floor and benches several times a day. (In very dry regions the space beneath the benches could be surfaced with 3 inches of coke, broken into pieces about 1 inch in diameter, which will absorb water when wet down with the hose and give it up gradually from innumerable evaporating surfaces.) Therefore it is obvious that to do a good job it is necessary to take the weather into consideration. (See discussion of Humidity in Chapter 2.)

CLEANLINESS

Although on the whole it is better to avoid overwetting of the leaves, it is desirable to spray them occasionally, say about every two weeks, to cleanse them of dust and thus improve their appearance. This periodic spraying is also a helpful measure against mites and insects. The water, a few degrees higher than air temperature, should be applied as a fine spray with considerable force. Syringing nozzles especially designed for this purpose are available. Syringing should be done when the air is fairly dry, preferably on a cloudy day, to lessen the danger of ring spot. It should be remembered that the spores of disease, if any are present, can be spread by syringing. Regular spraying, about every week or ten days, against insect pests and mites is a desirable preventive procedure.

Maintaining the house in a clean condition is important. Dying leaves, faded flowers, and spent flower stalks should be picked off daily, put in a paper bag, removed, and burned. The space beneath the benches should be kept free and clear. Under no circumstances should pots containing dead plants be thrown there, no matter how great the temptation.

If you make it a practice to transfer the plants to the porch or outdoors during the summer, take advantage of the opportunity presented by an empty house and give it a thorough cleaning. Remove the covering of sand or gravel from the benches and replace with new materials after the interior—glass, roof bars, and walls—has been washed down with soapy water. Spray plants with Isotox just before putting them inside from a summer outside.

Soil Storage   Before winter sets in, enough soil for potting operations should be prepared, sterilized, and stored. Even easier is to buy prepared potting soils in big bales or mix a batch of your own formula with clean peat moss, vermiculite, perlite, etc.

CHAPTER 11

Propagation

The facility with which *Saintpaulia* can be propagated doubtless is one of the chief reasons for its phenomenal spread as a house plant. Raising new plants of African-violets from leaf cuttings is as easy as eating pie; from stem cuttings of side shoots or offsets it is a little more difficult, but blooms come earlier than from leaf cuttings. Divisions of multiple-crown plants may be in bloom a month or six weeks after the operation which, however, may not be 100 per cent successful unless carefully done. Raising African-violets from seeds demands know-how, care in carrying out the various steps, and patience—you probably will have to wait nine months or so for the first bloom, and another year before the real character of the plant is evident.

LEAF CUTTINGS

Leaves can be rooted at any season, but the preferred time is early spring. If they are inserted then, plants of flowering size will usually be produced to give a good display during the following winter.

Mature but not aging leaves should be chosen, and, of course, taken from healthy plants unless it is a case of attempting to save a special variety suffering from incurable root or stem disease. Remove leaves from the plant with a sideways jerk so that no stub is left behind to decay and possibly start trouble. Then, with a sharp knife, cut off the stalk about 1½ inches from the base of the blade. Leaves will produce plantlets if longer or shorter stalks are left, but usually better results are obtained when cut as suggested above.

Every grower has his own preferred procedure from this step on. My pet method is to put them in a discarded aquarium containing 3 inches of a mixture of 2 parts sand and 1 part peat moss. A hole is made 1¼ inches deep with a finger, the leaf-stalk is inserted diagonally with the top side of the leaf up, and the sand and peat moss are pressed down gently around the base of the stalk. When all the leaves are inserted, they are watered with tepid water and from then on kept moist and out of direct sunshine. Other ways of arriving at the same end in the Free home include insertion in flats, flowerpots, or pans, using the same rooting material or vermiculite, or root them in water.

Humidity   No cover is needed to maintain moist air around the cuttings in the aquarium; neither is one necessary if the cuttings are put in during the season when no artificial heat is used. But in houses where the air is excessively dry, some device should be used to moisten the air in their vicinity. This may be a drinking glass inverted over the leaves when they are in a container small enough to permit this, or a glass bowl could be used to cover a 6- or 8-inch bulb pan. They may be covered with a wrapping of cellophane or waxed paper, or they may be put in a flowerpot with only a couple of inches of rooting medium in the bottom so that the leaves are below the rim on which a piece of glass can be laid. Very little watering is needed (after the initial one) when the cuttings are completely covered. If moisture condenses on the cover to such an extent that it may drip on the leaves, it should be tilted, or, in the case of cellophane, a few holes punched in it.

Time Lapse   Leaf cuttings vary greatly in the time required to produce plants large enough for transplanting. This is conditioned by season of insertion, maturity of the leaves, and nature of the variety. The average is about four months; one grower claims ten to twelve weeks. On the other hand, some are very slow—I have leaves of two varieties started in March which rooted normally but did not begin to form plantlets until September.

Transplanting   The number of plantlets produced by each leaf may vary from one to five, or even more. They are ready to be transplanted when the largest has leaves 2 or 3 inches long. Whether to separate them at this stage depends partly on the number (if more than three it is better to divide them) and partly on whether single- or multiple-crown plants are preferred. Remove the cuttings from the rooting medium with roots intact, shake to remove surplus soil, and then gently pull the plantlets apart.

They should then be potted separately in 2¼- or 3-inch pots (according to size of plantlets) in a mixture of equal parts soil, sand, peat moss or leafmold. If the soil is clayey, increase the amount of sand. The commercial soil-free mixes which do not contain a heavy dose of fertilizers are suitable for plantlets, as are the formulas sold as propagating or sowing mixes. Plantlets which have a sizable root system should be hand potted; smaller ones can be dibbled in by making a hole in the soil with a finger or pointed stick. The original leaf can be discarded, or it can be potted to continue producing plantlets if more are needed.

When the plantlets are not separated at potting time, the usual practice is to cut off the original leaf at soil level and either throw it away or reinsert it to continue working.

Variations   As previously hinted, every grower has a favorite method of rooting leaves. I suppose most amateurs start them in water, a method I am not too keen about because when they are withdrawn there is a tendency for the roots to mat together in rattails like those seen on the head of a straight-haired girl when she emerges from a swim. This means that they are bunched

(*Top left*) *New plants grown from a leaf cutting after 4½ months' time. The original leaf is still lusty.*

(*Top right*) *Here is what division of the potful disclosed—three infant plants and their mother. All the offspring developed at the base of the old petiole.*

(*Middle*) *The largest of the three plantlets is big enough to be potted by hand.*

(*Bottom*) *The whole family nearly ready to go; all that remains is to finish planting the baby.*

when potted instead of being naturally dispersed in the soil, unless you are willing to go to the trouble of filling a baking pan with water, standing an empty pot in it, putting in the rooted cutting with the roots supported by the water, and then pouring soil around them, as suggested by a writer in the *African Violet Magazine.*

There are many who advocate stretching a piece of waxed paper over a drinking glass, holding it in place with a rubber band, and then punching a hole in it through which the leafstalk is passed, the idea being to keep the leaf blade from contact with the water in the tumbler. This has never worked well for me—the top-heavy leaves always have a tendency to lie flat and heave the bases of the stalks out of the water. For starting leaves in water, I much prefer to use small cheese glasses. In these 1 inch of water is maintained and the leaves are supported by the side walls.

A modified water-started method involves the use of a soup plate or cereal bowl in which the leaf blades are rested on the edge and small pebbles are put in the bottom to hold the bases in place. Enough water is then put in to reach almost to the leaf blades.

A well-rooted cutting in water (left) discloses tiny leaves growing just below the water line. The leaf cutting being held (right) has been rooted in water; those to the left, in sand-leafmold-soil mixture; to the right, in vermiculite under a glass lid on the container.

Water-started leaves should be potted just as soon as plantlets begin to appear at the base of the leafstalk.

Expanded mica (vermiculite) in a horticultural grade is a material preferred by many in place of sand or sand and peat moss and there is no doubt that its use results in a strong root system. On the basis of a single experiment I made, it would seem that watering the cuttings occasionally with vitamin B_1 solution (one $\frac{1}{25}$ milligram pellet to 1 gallon of water) is advantageous. Liquid SuperThrive is a commercial plant stimulant which contains vitamin B. Use SuperThrive, 1 to 4 drops per gallon of room-temperature water.

Commercial growers commonly use coarse sand (or vermiculite) in their propagating benches in which the cuttings are inserted row after row after row. Some of them are eliminating one handling by inserting the leaves directly in $2\frac{1}{4}$-inch pots (from which they will be sold) in African-violet soil to which sand has been added to make it more porous. When the plantlets start, liquid fertilizer is used to promote quick growth. Home growers could adapt this method to their own use by pressing the pots into moist sand, using a system of constant water-level watering as described in Chapter 6. Unless some such scheme is used, difficulty would be experienced under home conditions in maintaining the soil in the desirable constantly moist condition.

There is no end to the kind of containers that can be put to use. In addition to those mentioned, coffee cans, waxed cardboard cottage-cheese or ice-cream containers, fish bowls, terrariums, and candy dishes have been used. Choose the one which is most conveniently accessible to you.

STEM CUTTINGS OF OFFSETS

In the course of their growth, saintpaulias develop side shoots or offsets from the base of the crown, the number varying in accordance with the variety, some being much more prolific than others. If these are left, usually they ultimately will develop their own root systems and form multiple-crowned plants which can be propagated by division. Those who prefer single-crown plants either remove the offsets as soon as they are visible, or, if they need material for propagation, wait until the larger leaves are 2 or 3 inches long, when the offsets can be cut off and inserted as stem cuttings, which will root in three or four weeks and produce plants from which blooms may be expected in about five months.

Before starting to take off the cuttings it is desirable to have the soil a little on the dry side so that the leaves are less brittle and thus less likely to be broken when manipulating them to reach the offsets. Carefully lift, or part, the leaves with one hand and then, with a sharp, narrow-blade knife, cut off the offset close to the parent stem. The base of each cutting is then inserted in an individual pot containing one or other of the materials used in rooting leaves. I prefer regular African-violet soil modified by doubling the normal amount of sand. Some of the cuttings will have enough stem attached so that they can be held rigid by pressing the soil around them; others will have to be supported by two or more toothpicks stuck beside them in the soil. Water thoroughly, cover each pot with an inverted drinking glass or equivalent, and keep shaded from sun until rooted.

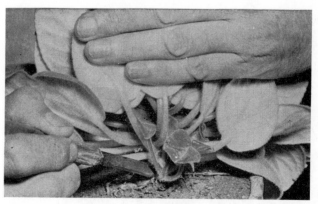

A more rapid method of increasing your stock is found in the small offsets that form from the main crown. These can be severed with a sharp knife.

DIVISION

Division is the quickest means of obtaining sizable new plants. If done at the right time—just after a resting period during which no blooms are produced and just as the crowns are starting new growth—flowers may be expected in about a month. The soil should be slightly on the dry side before starting the operation so that the leaves are not so brittle and therefore less likely to be broken and so that the root ball can be broken apart with greater ease. Usually no more than three new plants are obtainable by this method. It is a surgical operation with an element of risk, for sometimes one or more of the divisions dies, either because lack of care resulted in its removal with too few roots, or because organisms causing decay obtained entrance to the plant by way of the wounds.

Plants are ready for division when they have two or more crowns which have more or less grown apart at the base and rooted separately. As mentioned above, the best time to do the job is at the close of a resting period; but newly purchased multiple-crowned plants which have been grown with their roots crowded in 2¼- or 2½-inch pots usually should be divided within a few weeks after their receipt, whenever that may be.

Four offsets inserted in sand and peat mixture, the two smaller ones supported by toothpicks. The inverted tumbler maintains humidity around cutting; important if room air is dry.

The plant to be divided is removed from the pot by turning it upside down and tapping the rim on the edge of the bench or table, not forgetting to cover the soil with the fingers of one hand to prevent it from spilling and to keep the plant from falling to the floor.

The next step is to shake off loose soil from sides and top of root ball and place the plant on its side on the table to enable you to see more clearly where the crowns are attached to each other. If necessary, they are cut apart with a sharp knife and then gently and carefully the divisions are pulled apart, making every effort to permit each division to retain its full quota of roots.

The pots should be washed and the soil prepared and sterilized (see Chapter 5) ahead of time so that there is no unnecessary delay which might result in drying and death of outer roots. The drainage material (if any is used) is put in the bottom of the pot, followed by a handful of soil lightly pressed down with the fingers, and the division centered in the pot with the point of attachment of lowermost leaves ½ inch below the rim. Soil is then filled in around the roots, lightly firmed, and brought up to within ½ inch of the rim, taking care not to cover the crown of central leaves with soil.

PLANTS FROM SEEDS

Starting African-violets from seeds is one of the most interesting projects it is possible to undertake in house-plant culture. It is fascinating to watch their germination—first, the minute needle-like shoots of green, then the unfolded cotyledons, barely $\frac{1}{16}$ of an inch across, followed by the true foliage leaves, which, however, lack the conspicuous venation characteristic of mature plants. You can purchase seeds from dealers but you won't know ahead of time what the seedlings will be like in terms of flower color, size, and shape, or habit of the plants which, in a way, makes it all the more interesting. The process is still more cap-

These tiny African-violets are two-month-old seedlings.

tivating if you start from scratch, act the part of a marriage broker and obtain the seeds from your own saintpaulias though you still will not know ahead what the progeny will look like, unless perhaps you self-pollinate species such as *S. ionantha* and *S. diplotricha,* the seedlings of which may be expected closely to resemble their parents.

What Will You Get?   This is not the place to delve deeply into Mendel's law of inheritance. Briefly you can expect that most of the first-generation seedlings from crossing two varieties will resemble the pistil parent (mother) rather than the pollen parent (father); and a few may be different from either mother or father. By crossing two of your best plants you *may* have something worth keeping in the first generation of seedlings; by crossing the best of these, and by self-pollinating some, you stand a chance of getting something really good. But, as you can readily see, this involves raising hundreds of seedlings and discarding most of them, so here is a warning: Don't raise African violets from seeds unless you have plenty of room to accommodate the progeny when they grow up—or can discard the surplus without tearing your heartstrings.

According to Dr. P. J. Greenway of Tanzania (the native home of the African-violet), as quoted in the *National Horticultural Magazine,* "They do set seeds in the wild but not very freely."

I have seldom seen fully developed seed pods on a cultivated African-violet, except those from flowers which had been artificially pollinated. Occasionally a pod will develop without artificial aid on some varieties—I have seen such on 'Viking' and 'Commodore'—but in order to get seeds it is necessary to perform a few manipulations. Let's look into the why and how of this.

A close-up of the flowers show that the styles veer off to the right or left, well away from the pollen-bearing anthers. This probably is a device to prevent self-pollination. Actually, it would seem, in view of the report that African-violets do not in nature set seeds freely, that they not only avoid self-pollination

Each blossom has a single style or stalk, with the stigma at its tip, veering off to one side. In the center are the two-lobed anthers which bear pollen.

but also to a large extent make it difficult to secure cross-pollination. (The style is the stalk of the pistil. At its base is the ovary containing ovules which, when fertilized, develop into seeds; at its tip is the stigma, a tiny knob on which the pollen grains germinate to effect fertilization.)

The pollen is produced in two 2-lobed anthers placed back to back. When the ripe anthers are pulled apart with tweezers, a little puff of pollen escapes, and more is visible within the irregularly shaped, craterlike opening on the back of each anther. One can imagine that in the wild some kind of an insect occasionally finds his way into a floral opening, wanders between the anthers, and in so doing becomes dusted with the pollen. Then in approaching another flower he comes in contact with its stigma and effects its pollination. (Under cultivation, thrips are reputed occasionally to be the agents in effecting pollination.)

How to Pollinate While the way in which pollination is achieved in nature is speculative, we do know how it can be done with plants growing in our homes, and various means which can be adopted are described in the pages which follow.

1. The simplest way is to place a finger (wash and dry hands first) beneath the anthers and crush them down on it with the

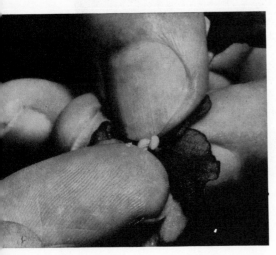

To cross-pollinate African-violets, transfer the pollen from anther to stigma by hand. To do this, place a thumb or fingertip under the anthers and crush them with your other thumbnail.

thumbnail of the other hand. This results in a deposit of pollen on the finger which is in turn gently smeared on the stigma of the flower selected to be the female parent.

2. A larger quantity of pollen can be obtained if the anthers are cut off with nail scissors and separated by pulling them apart over a piece of black paper—black so that the white pollen can be seen easily. If the anthers are teased, tapped, and shaken with tweezers, still more pollen will be obtained. A modification of this method is to slice off the tips of the anthers with a razor blade or sharp scissors and then proceed as suggested above. The transfer of pollen to the stigma is accomplished by shaking (or brushing with a small camel's-hair brush) the pollen together near an edge of the paper and then bending a flower over so that the stigma can be dipped in it. Alternatively, the pollen can be taken up on a finger and applied to the stigma as in method number one.

3. An anther may be gently pulled part from its mate with tweezers and the stigma dipped in the pollen exposed in the opening on its back, or an anther with its tip sliced off may similarly be applied to the stigma.

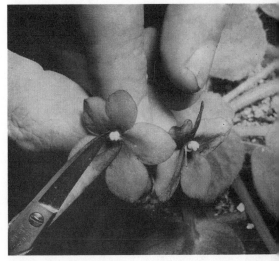

More pollen can be obtained if you snip off the anthers with sharp-pointed scissors just below the junction with their supporting stems.

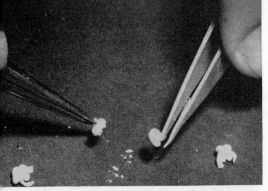

After the anthers have been clipped off, they can be pulled apart with two pairs of forceps, releasing some of the pollen onto a sheet of black paper.

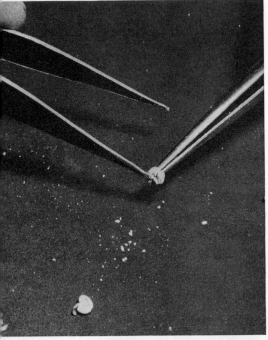

Poking the anther with the point of one of the forceps releases a little more pollen. Note the irregular, craterlike opening on the back of each anther which furnishes the escape route for the pollen.

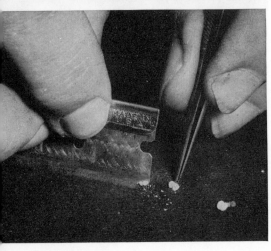

A modification of the method shown in the two preceding photos is to expose the pollen cavities by slicing off the tips of the anthers with a razor blade.

After collecting the pollen on black paper, gently brush the grains together near one side of the paper and carry them to the blossom to be fertilized.

Another pollination method is to take the anther directly to the stigma of the blossom selected as the female parent.

You will have to decide which of these methods best fits your preferences and capabilities. Number one is the easiest and, if only one or two flowers are to be pollinated, is probably the best. Number two makes more pollen available and is desirable when you propose to pollinate several flowers. Number three I like the least—perhaps because it demands steadier hands than I possess; then, too, edged tools are dangerous in some hands! I've tried all methods and have had successes and failures with all. The failures I attribute to the use of flowers either too old or too young. It seems to me that the best results are obtained when

Results of fertilization should be apparent when the ovaries begin to swell (center of photograph, at six-weeks stage).

mature but not fading flowers are used both to provide pollen and to receive it.

After a week or so, if fertilization has been effected, the ovaries will begin to swell. I failed to note when my first pollinations were made, but I think it was late one winter, say about the first of March. Three flowers were pollinated. The first pod was ripe on June 4, the second on July 8, the third on July 20, on which date the seeds from all the capsules were separately sown. This gives a period of four to five and a half months from pollination to harvest. Others say six to nine months are necessary, and they may be right. The capsules are ready for removal when the stem withers. Put in a paper envelope and, after three weeks, open capsules, remove seeds, and sow them.

Sowing the Seeds   I sowed these seeds with the aid of an iced-tea spoon at three stations on the surface of a sifted (⅛-inch sieve), moist mixture of sand and old leafmold (equal parts) contained

Seeds can be sown in a square Mason jar. In this case the soil is filled to the level of the opening and smoothed and compacted with an old table knife. A round jar is not suitable unless securely braced to prevent disturbing the seed bed.

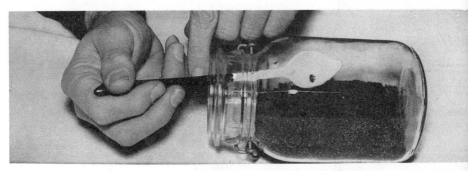

The seeds are sown from a kitchen spoon, tilted slightly and continually tapped to jar out the seeds gradually as it is moved around over the soil.

in a square Mason jar. It was placed on its side and filled to the level of the opening with soil which was smoothed and patted down with a table knife. The mixture was not sterilized, though doubtless it would have been safer to do so. After the seeds were sown, without any soil covering, the lid was put on the jar without the rubber ring. Usually germination takes place before it is necessary to apply additional water; but if the soil should show signs of becoming dry, water may be given by gently spooning it in. (Incidentally, I have come to the conclusion that this manner of sowing, recommended by several African-violet growers, has

Well-sifted sand and peat moss, plus ⅓ teaspoon of ground lime-stone, comprise the seed-sowing mixture. When these ingredients have been mixed, place them in a flowerpot drained with broken pot pieces and moss.

When the pot has been filled to the rim, the surface of the mixture is leveled off by drawing a piece of straight-edged wood across. Then a small tamper is used to press the mixture down about ¼ inch below the rim.

Seeds are sown evenly by shaking them from a paper packet. Labeling data are written on a strip of adhesive pressed firmly against the side of the pot.

Next, the pot is placed in a saucer and covered with a glass coaster to prevent evaporation. All watering is done from below by placing the water in the saucer, where it rises to moisten the surface soil.

no advantage over the orthodox method, which makes use of an ordinary seed pan or pot covered with glass. Actually, it is a little more difficult to sow the seeds and to remove the seedlings from the jar than it is from a seed pan.)

The seeds which ripened on July 8 came up like hair on a dog's back on August 1; there was sparse germination of the other two (June 4 and July 20) on August 21. Whether or not the time lapse between ripening and sowing has any bearing on the time of germination and the number of seedlings I am not prepared to say. There may be other factors involved. Jessie Crawford, reporting in *The Home Garden,* says that seeds planted three weeks after ripening will germinate in about two weeks; if they are sown immediately, germination may take nine months.

Transplanting Half of the seedlings from the good stand were dug up with a teaspoon and transplanted sixteen days after germination. The seedlings at this stage were so tiny that this was a ticklish job—more so as I was watched by several kibitzers who happened to drop in and by the photographer, who was anxious to get on with the next picture. Good eyes, steady hands, and a mechanical aid in the form of a transplanting fork are necessary to do the work properly.

Individual seedlings were picked out from the clump by slip-
ping a transplanting fork beneath the cotyledons and lifting. The
transplanting fork was made by whittling down the pointed end
of a 6-inch wooden pot label to a thin sliver and then cutting a
V-shaped notch in it. As soon as the transplanting was finished
(in this instance, working against time, not all the seedlings
were transplanted), the soil was settled around the roots by
spraying it with a fine spray. The soil used was a sifted mixture

*Two weeks after germination the
tiny seedlings are ladled out with
a teaspoon. If additional water
is needed in the jar, it can be applied with a spoon.*

*A transplanting fork is used to
remove the seedlings individually
from the clump and set them in
a new bed where they can be
well spaced.*

of 2 parts sand, 1 part leafmold (or peat moss), and 1 part soil, the upper half inch being passed through a ⅛-inch screen.

The other half of the seedlings were transplanted when they were three months old, averaging about an inch across with four or five true leaves. The only advantage of waiting until they are of this size is that transplanting is easier, but many of the seedlings (which could have been saved if transplanted early) are killed by being crowded by strong-growing neighbors. Excessive vigor is not necessarily a good attribute.

One of the charms of raising African-violets from seed is that, especially when two distinct varieties are crossed, you do not know what you are going to get until the progeny comes to maturity. You may get a bunch of mediocrities; on the other hand, you *may* get some plants that are more beautiful than any African-violets you have ever seen before. But for pity's sake, don't name any and put them on the market unless you are very sure they are superior to already-existing named varieties—already there are too many inferior varieties that never should have been awarded the dignity of a distinguishing name.

A fine spray of water is used to settle the soil around the roots of the newly set seedlings.

Some seedling comparisons. The plant in the rear is two years old; those in the foreground are three months. Those at the right, transplanted when about two weeks old, are stronger than their sisters at the left, which have just been set out.

Young Plants or Old? Although plants may remain healthy and floriferous for a number of years, many of the plants of some varieties deteriorate after two or three years. It is a good plan to raise young stock annually to take the place of those suffering from senility.

REGISTRATION OF NEW HYBRIDS

The African Violet Society of America, as the international authority for registration of *Saintpaulia,* issues the following information regarding registration procedures:

INFORMATION AND INSTRUCTIONS
CONCERNING REGISTRATION AND NAME
RESERVATIONS OF AFRICAN VIOLETS

REGISTRATION

REGISTRATION is a public claim to having originated a new and worthy variety of African Violet (it is not a certification by the Society that the variety is new and different). Send a request to the Registrar for the number of REGISTRATION CARDS needed. Registration is accomplished by filling out one card (typewritten if possible) for each plant to be registered. The applicant keeps one card for his or her file. Applicant must date and sign the card and mail it back first class to the Registrar. Do not bend or fold the card. Please accompany the card with the proper fee. The Registrar checks the card for completeness of information and apparent corrections; if it appears in order it will then be included in the Registrar's quarterly report, and published in a subsequent issue of the *African Violet Magazine*.

Check the card before sending. Complete color variations must be given, also a complete description of the foliage. Each of the spaces on the card should be checked. The code that is printed in the magazine is made up from the information given by you on the card. This code is used by the Judges when judging all local and convention shows. The code is also used in our judging schools. IT MUST BE CORRECT.

The A.V.S. is required to abide by the INTERNATIONAL CODE OF NOMENCLATURE FOR CULTIVATED PLANTS; for example—
The variety names must contain only one or two words and in no case have more than three words.
Names beginning with abbreviations except Mrs. must be avoided. All variety names must be written out in full, such as Mount Kisco, not Mt. Kisco; not St. Louis but Saint Louis.
Names containing excessively long words or phrases will not be accepted. Be safe, send your names in for reservation before releasing the variety. The name can then be changed if it is not acceptable.

REGISTRATION CARDS must be received on or before—

SEPTEMBER	28	to	be	published	in	JAN.	AVSA Magazine
NOVEMBER	28	"	"	"	"	MAR.	AVSA Magazine
FEBRUARY	28	"	"	"	"	JUNE	AVSA Magazine
MAY	28	"	"	"	"	SEPT.	AVSA Magazine
JULY	28	"	"	"	"	NOV.	AVSA Magazine

Registrations are not considered registered or eligible for AVSA awards until published in the African Violet Society Inc. Magazine.

Registrations must be received on or before November 28 to be eligible for the annual AVSA Convention Awards.

By action of the Board of Directors of the African Violet Society at the Nashville convention of 1953 a $3.00 registration fee was set for each registration application. This must be sent to the Registrar along with the Application for Registration.

NAME RESERVATION

The reason for Name Reservation can be explained as follows:

Since registration requires that a plant be carried through at least three generations, it has frequently occurred that a name honestly applied to a plant by one person during the testing period was selected by others and used for registration before the testing was completed. Meanwhile some specimens of said plant under test had been sold under the name. The hybridizer sends the Application for Registration in at the end of the testing period, and the Registrar must refuse to accept the application as there is another plant registered under the name you have selected. This can be prevented by reserving the name you plan to use before placing the plant on the market.

There is no card to be filled out by the applicant for name reservation. All that is necessary is to write the Registrar stating that you have a promising plant or plants and would like to reserve your selected names for them. By action of the Board of Directors of the AVSA, Inc. at the Nashville convention in 1953 a fee of $1.00 was set for each name reserved for a period of two years. This may be applied to the $3.00 fee at the time of registration. This fee must accompany each request for name reservation. The Registrar will check the files and inform you of the status of the names you have selected. These names will then be placed on file under your name for a period of two years. Renewals of reservations are subject to an additional fee of $1.00 for another period of two years.

Responsibility of the Society for a name reservation ends with publication of reservation in the *African Violet Magazine.* The Society has no power to enforce observation of a reservation. However, under no circumstance will another plant be registered under the name reserved so long as the reservation has not expired. The two-year period starts at the time of publication in the AVSA Magazine.

The above information, reproduced as received from the AVSA, provides full details regarding how to register new hybrids. To keep cultivars correctly labeled, it is wise to officially register any new hybrid that will be propagated and distributed but use special restraint to only introduce hybrids that are improvements over existing types. The official form for saintpaulia registration is reproduced on the following page.

APPLICATION FOR REGISTRATION

African Violet Society of America, Inc.

NAME PROPOSED	REGISTRATION NO. (LEAVE BLANK)	
		DATE RECEIVED_____
		DATE PUBLISHED_____

APPLICANT'S NAME AND ADDRESS | ORIGINATOR'S NAME AND ADDRESS

ORIGIN

☐ SEEDLING ☐ SPORT

PARENTS OF SEEDLING OR ORIGIN OF SPORT OR MUTATION

☐ MUTATION BY CHEMICALS ☐ MUTATION BY RADIATION

NO. GENERATIONS PROPAGATED

☐ NEW VARIETY
☐ IMPROVED VARIETY
(NAME OF VARIETY) _____

ADDITIONAL COMMENTS:

BLOSSOM DESCRIPTION

MAIN COLOR ON FACE | COLOR VARIATIONS (WHERE) | COLOR OF PETAL BACK | LENGTH OF MATUR

☐ SINGLE ☐ DOUBLE
☐ STAR ☐ FRINGED OR RUFFLED

AVERAGE SIZE OF BLOOM (INCHES)

☐ SLOW BLOOMER
☐ PROLIFIC BLOOMER

AVERAGE NO. IN CL

ADDITIONAL COMMENTS:

LEAF DESCRIPTION

COLOR ON TOP | COLOR ON LEAF REVERSE

☐ LONGIFOLIA OR SPIDER ☐ GIRL ☐ VARIGATED ☐ POINTED LEAF ☐ HAIRY

☐ PLAIN ☐ RUFFLED, FRINGED, WAVY OR SCALLOPED ☐ SPOONED ☐ GLOSSY ☐ OTHER

☐ QUILTED ☐ SUPREME OR DU PONT ☐ OVATE OR CUPPED UP   WHY_____

ADDITIONAL COMMENTS:

GROWTH HABIT

DIAMETER OF MATURE PLANT
☐ 6" OR UNDER ☐ 8" IN" THROUGH 16"
☐ 6" THROUGH 8" ☐ OVER 16"

FORM ☐ UPRIGHT ☐ DROOPY ☐ FLAT WHEEL ☐ OTHER _____

ADDITIONAL COMMENTS:

DATE OF APPLICATION_____ SIGNATURE _____

Two copies of this form are provided. The Applicant keeps one. The other copy should be filled out on the typewriter, dated, si
the Applicant, and mailed First Class to the Chairman of Registration. Do not bend or fold this card. Place additional comments
the space provided, or on extra sheet of paper. Do not print or write in other spaces. Please accompany this application with pro

REVISED JULY 1, 1964

CHAPTER 12

Species
and Varieties
of Saintpaulia

Because so many African-violet enthusiasts are under the impression that they are the African representatives of true Violets, which they definitely are not, it is desirable to attempt to indicate the place of these two groups in relation to each other.

Saintpaulia belongs in the Gesneria family (*Gesneriaceae*) which also includes ornamental genera such as *Achimenes, Columnea, Corytholoma, Conandron, Episcia, Haberlea, Kohleria, Petrocosmea, Ramonda, Sinningia (Gloxinia), Smithiantha,* and *Streptocarpus.* Of these, *Ramonda,* native to the Pyrenees, Serbia, et cetera, and *Haberlea,* which grows wild in the Balkans, can endure considerable freezing weather, and perhaps there is a remote possibility that a hybrid could be obtained between *Saintpaulia* and one or the other of them and, as a result, a plant with *Saintpaulia* characteristics which might thrive under cool temperatures. The very rare *Petrocosmea kerri* from Siam could, in a photograph of it I have seen, easily be mistaken for a *Saintpaulia*—it has the same general shape of leaves, same hairiness, and same type of flowers. The latter are white and "the upper petals are *distinctively marked with bright yellow.*" This species might give hybridizers an opportunity to introduce the longed-for (by some) yellow coloring into the petals of *Saintpaulia.* If any of the scarlet-flowered Episcias would hybridize with *Saintpaulia,* it might be possible to produce an African-violet with flowers that are really red. But bi-generic hybrids are rare and the outlook is not very promising, because of genetic incompatibility.

The Violets of our woods and fields and the Pansies of our gardens belong in an entirely different and not even related plant family, the *Violaceae,* far removed botanically from the *Gesneriaceae.* So far as I know, inter-family hybrids have never been made so those who attempt to hybridize yellow Violets with *Saintpaulia* are just wasting their time.

Botanists have classified plants on the basis of their apparent relationship. We can for our purpose ignore the larger groupings of divisions, classes, orders, et cetera, and concentrate on family, genus, species, varieties, and clones. A plant family consists of genera (plural of genus) which have a family resemblance. For instance, the Carrot family (*Umbelliferae*) includes, among many others, Carrot, Parsley, Celery, and Parsnip, all of which produce their flowers in umbels. A *genus* is a group of plants more like each other than any other group; there is closer resemblance between the members of a genus than between the members of two families. A *species* is a group of individuals more like each other than any other group within a genus. Usually seeds of a species will develop into plants which closely resemble their parent. A *variety,* botanically, is a group of plants within a species which have constant characters causing them to differ slightly from the species. Horticulturally the term is applied to variants which may come as a result of continued selection, by crossing, or by mutation. (This last term is applied to changes in character not owing to crossing.)

Mutants (also known as "sports" or "breaks") occur frequently among seedlings and, especially in the case of *Saintpaulia,* as bud sports from leaf cuttings. An environment different from that which the species experiences in nature may sometimes be the compelling cause for alteration of the genes (inheritance factors), which results in mutation. Sometimes the mutations are stable and sometimes they revert back to the original.

Clone is the term applied to a group of plants which have

been propagated without recourse to seeds from a plant raised from seeds. For example, *Saintpaulia* variety 'Helen Wilson' originated as a seedling; the plants propagated from it by leaf cuttings are clones.

Cultivar is a specific term used to designate clones that are found mainly in cultivation. Technically a new hybrid or species mutation propagated vegetatively is a cultivar.

SAINTPAULIA SPECIES

Saintpaulia, then, is a genus in the Gesneria family. The number of species contained in the genus is not certainly known, but at least twenty species have been named, most from Tanzania, where they range from near sea level to about 7,000 feet. Brief descriptions of the best-known species follow. The name appearing after the species name is that of the authority responsible for the name of that particular species.

Saintpaulia diplotricha, B. L. Burtt. Pale green leaves, almost white on the undersides; in outline, elliptic to oval almost rounded at the tip, with cordate (heart-shaped) base and wavy margins (shallowly crenate in my plant). Sometimes the plant has a tendency to make a short, thick, creeping stem. The 1¼-inch flowers are freely produced, about three to a stalk; the upper petals tend to fold back lengthwise, giving the flowers a perky look. Their color is medium blue-violet in the shade and violet, a shade darker, in sun. Mr. Burtt, who described this species, distinguishes it from *S. ionantha* by the the long and short hairs which clothe the leaves as compared with those of uniform length which are found in *S. ionantha.* A further distinction is in the fruits (seed capsules), which are long and curved (sometimes) in *S. diplotricha* and short in *S. ionantha.* The leaves are comparatively thin. It is distinct from other saintpaulias. It was formerly known as *S. kewensis* under which name it was sold by many American dealers. East Usambara Mountains, 1,000 to about 3,000 feet.

Saintpaulia diplotricha *has handsome foliage, nearly white on the undersides, and perky medium blue-violet flowers.*

Saintpaulia goetzeana, Engler. Somewhat densely white-hairy. Stems elongate from 4 to 6 inches long with several pairs of opposite leaves ½ to 1 inch apart. Leaves as those of *S. kewensis.* Peduncles solitary, axillary, ½ to 1½ inches long, one to three flowered. Flowers nearly like those of *S. kewensis* but the corolla lobes more unequal, the two posticous much shorter than the others. Mozambique, Uluguru. Lakwangula Plateau, 4,000 to 6,300 feet. (Description from *Flora of Tropical Africa,* Thistleton Dyer, 1906.) This species has opposite leaves.

Saintpaulia grotei, Engler. This species has glossy almost round leaves, heart-shaped at base often with an overlapping lobe; pale green above, whitish beneath; older leaves with stalks up to 10 inches, only sparsely hairy; shallow crenations (Roberts says "dentate") which tend to disappear as the leaf ages; young petioles red-brown. The flowers, two or three to a stalk

S. grotei *has long, creeping stems which show to good advantage in a hanging basket or tall container, as shown here. The flowers are pale blue-violet.*

(usually four on my plant), are pale blue-violet deepening in color toward the center. The striking character of *S. grotei* is its long, creeping stems. Amani, 3,000 feet. Fully described and illustrated by Harvey Cox and Evan Roberts in the *African Violet Magazine,* Vol. 3, No. 3; used by breeders to develop trailing hybrids.

S. ionantha *is a free-blooming species which is easy to grow and as attractive as many of the newer varieties developed from it. Its petioles and the undersides of its leaves are sometimes flushed with rose.*

Saintpaulia ionantha, H. Wendland. Plants under cultivation allocated to this species are variable. This is the principal species used to create modern *Saintpaulia* hybrids. In general, the leaf-stalks are very long, the blades ovate, sub-cordate at base, crenate, obtuse at the tip; rather densely covered with hairs mostly of uniform length; surface somewhat lustrous and quilted. Petioles and undersides of leaves sometimes flushed with rose. Pale-violet flowers, 1¼ to 1½ inches, 3 to 8 on each stalk rising to top of foliage. Seed capsules short and fat. Tanzania, near sea level, 50 to 300 feet.

Saintpaulia kewensis, C. B. Clarke. See *S. diplotricha.*

Saintpaulia magungensis, E. P. Roberts. New species described and named by E. P. Roberts in the *African Violet Magazine,* Vol. 3, No. 4, 1950. Habit of growth similar to that of *S. grotei,* the difference being much smaller crenate leaves on shorter stalks and smaller, darker violet-blue flowers, with

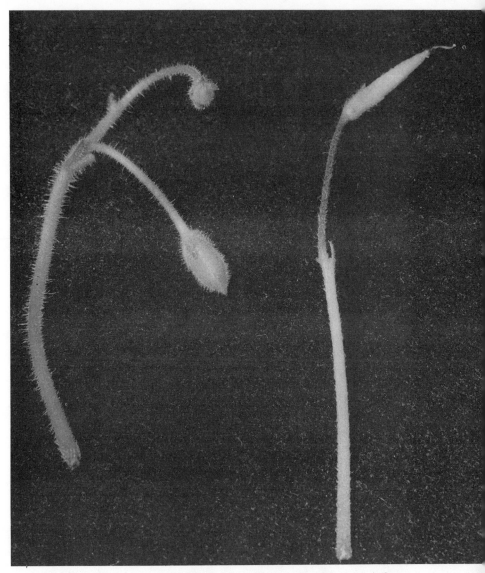

To distinguish some of the Saintpaulia *species, compare the size and shape of the seed capsules.* S. ionantha (*left*) *has short, fat seed capsules.* S. diplotricha (*right*) *has long, slender capsules, which sometimes are also decidedly curved.*

deeper color in center. Magunga, foothills Usambara Mountains. A small growing variety is called *S. magungensis minima* and the species formally known as *S. amaniensis* is now included under the species *S. magungensis*.

Saintpaulia orbicularis, B. L. Burtt. Leaves round in outline, cordate at the base. Flowers smaller than those of *S. ionantha,* more numerous; white with lavender ring around anthers; underside of petals white with light crimson veins; tips washed with same color. Sakarre, Ambangula, about 3,900 feet.

Saintpaulia pusilla, Engler. Similar to *S. ionantha,* Wendland, but smaller in every part. Leaf blade 1 by ⅔ inch, sparsely hairy, entire, purple beneath. Cymes small, few-flowered. Calyx lobes, ⅛ inch long. Corolla, ⅓ inch in diameter. Capsule, ⅓ by ⅟₁₂ inch. Mozambique, Uluguru. Lakwangula Plateau, 4,000 to 5,600 feet. (Description from *Flora of Tropical Africa,* Thistleton Dyer, 1906.)

Saintpaulia shumensis, B. L. Burtt. A miniature species with 1- to 1⅜-inch-long leaves, olive-green with erect hairs. Pale mauve to white flowers with violet blotch inside, up to five flowers per stalk. This species has been used to breed many of the modern miniatures. From West Usambara Mountains, around 5,900 feet above sea level.

Saintpaulia tongwensis, B. L. Burtt. Similar to *S. ionantha* but with longer, glossier, almost elliptical, non-quilted, shining leaves with a sub-acute tip. The midrib and main veins are dimly visible from above as pale green lines. The seed capsules are densely hairy and longer than those of *S. ionantha.*

Of the species listed above *S. diplotricha* (*kewensis*), *S. grotei, S. ionantha, S. magungensis, S. shumensis,* and *S. tongwensis* have been offered by commercial growers. Some of the others are sometimes available from specialists but are not easy to find in commercial catalogues.

On the basis of my limited experience with species, I would say that *S. diplotricha* is worth growing by those whose object is assembling a collection of saintpaulias that are *different.* It is not so showy as many, nor does it bloom over such long periods, but it is distinct. *S. grotei,* because of its trailing habit, has great possibilities as a plant for hanging pots or baskets. *S. ionantha* is a free, easy grower and can still hold its own with many of the newer varieties. *S. tongwensis* has not done well for me—it became afflicted with mites and, although it is free of them now, it has not fully recovered from the experience, but I believe it has possibilities.

Doubtless plant breeders will quickly get to work on these new species and try to hybridize them with each other and with existing varieties. If they are successful, we can look for immense changes in the appearance of saintpaulia varieties in the near future. *S. grotei* and others can be combined with the large-flowered, profuse-blooming varieties and we are already seeing innovations from breeders who have used *S. grotei* to produce trailing hybrids with large flowers, all welcome improvements in an already glamorous genus.

SAINTPAULIA VARIETIES

It must be remembered that saintpaulias are unstable "critters" so that it is practically impossible to describe them accurately and have the description stick. The flower color may vary according to the region, light conditions, and the soil in which they are grown; their size is influenced by the degree of culture given, the age of the plant, the season of year, and whether grown to single or multiple crowns. The way the flowers are held may depend on the stage of growth; sometimes the flower stalks are erect when they first emerge from the crown of leaves, becoming almost horizontal as they age. The general growth habit may vary also; at one stage most of the leaves will be held upright, but as the plant ages it may form a flattish rosette, or the leaves may even droop over the edge of the pot. This last condition has been attributed to exposure to low temperatures and to the roots being allowed to become too dry; but I feel sure that sometimes these factors are not responsible and one can only say it is the nature of the beast.

The leaves themselves differ in size and shape even on the same plant. Plants with lobed leaves after a few months may revert to regular, unlobed, almost round, leaves, as in the case of the variety 'Helen Wilson'. Mr. Frentzen, who was one of those responsible for the introduction of blue chard, told me of his embarrassment in being unable to supply plants of 'Helen Wilson' with lobed leaves because all of his stock had reverted. Spooning of leaves also is an inconstant character, and the conditions which determine it are mysterious. Sometimes it would seem that it is a matter of age and excellence of culture, but occasionally we come across young seedlings with spooned leaves, which become normal as the plant ages. There are some who believe that the spooning tendency is not reproduced in plants propagated by leaf cuttings but this has yet to be substantiated. The color of the undersides of the leaves is also unstable, varying with the season, exposure, and degree of maturity.

There is one sure thing we can say about saintpaulias—they are extremely variable.

Thousands of Varieties   The varieties of *Saintpaulia* run into the thousands. Some are very distinct; some have differences so minute that they are not worthy of a name; some are inferior and should be discarded; and many are definitely synonymous with other varieties. This is an unfortunate situation which has been accentuated by certain dealers who offer unnamed seedlings, giving the purchaser the privilege of naming them. It is easy to see where this kind of practice will lead—new names will be applied to varieties identical with some already named and many varieties unworthy to be perpetuated will receive a distinguishing name simply because the owner lacks the discernment properly to evaluate them. This condition will right itself to some extent as soon as devotees stop collecting just names; inferior varieties will be shunned by the purchasing public and thus they will go out of cultivation; and commercial growers in their own interests will drop those having constitutional defects which make them difficult to grow. However, one looks hopefully toward the Registration Committee of the African Violet Society to accelerate matters by reducing the duplicate names which probably run into hundreds and in encouraging a sense of responsibility among the breeders, which will deter them from naming inferior varieties.

(Editor's Note: As of 1977, more than 3,000 hybrids have been officially registered. Hundreds of new cultivars are introduced each year. C.M.F.)

Origin of Varieties The history of the development of saintpaulia varieties is obscure and uncertain. It would seem that two species—*S. diplotricha* and *S. ionantha*—were included in the original introduction of saintpaulia to cultivation and for a time both were known as *S. ionantha*. One would naturally suppose

'Mermaid' has medium blue, rather small flowers which are generously produced.

that, considering the favor with which they were received, gardeners would immediately have started hybridizing them to produce new kinds. But I cannot find any record of this; and a geneticist connected with the Montreal Botanic Garden, who is investigating *Saintpaulia* heredity, expressed the opinion that our present-day varieties had been developed from *S. ionantha*. At the time I found it hard to believe that *S. diplotricha* also did not enter into their make-up, but since then I have carefully looked for *S. diplotricha* traits in a hundred or more varieties without success, unless its influence is shown in the seed capsules of some varieties which are intermediate between those of *S. ionantha* and *S. diplotricha*.

As mentioned in Chapter 1, the varieties introduced by Armacost and Royston in 1926 provided the impetus culminating in the present-day rage for saintpaulias. 'Blue Boy' in particular captured the interest of the houseplant public because of its color, floriferousness, and ease of culture. It is still grown by some specialists.

It is obviously impossible to describe and evaluate all the varieties in a book such as this, so I propose first to discuss the various "groups," "strains," or "series," then list a dozen first-class, easily grown varieties followed by a listing of a few varieties which might be the objective of the grower with some experience. Although I have been assiduous in my endeavors to become acquainted with as many varieties as possible, I realize that doubtless there are many good ones omitted—either because I did not happen to see them or because they were not at their best at the time when they were viewed, and thus did not make an impression; or because they were not available for sale at the time of going to press.

(Editor's Note: In this revised edition of Mr. Free's classic book, I have included new material about modern hybrids. Our color photographs and the Official Top 25 African Violets List feature new hybrids available from commercial growers. C.M.F.)

'Amethyst Amazon' has 1½-inch flowers which are light red-violet at the margins and deepen toward the center. The leaves tend to "spoon." The detached leaf at left is from 'Amethyst'; at right, 'Amazon'.

CLASSIFICATION BY GROUPS

There are some varieties with certain characteristics in common —leaves with long petioles and comparatively small flowers, mostly in pale colors, which seem to be rather closely allied to *S. ionantha;* others with rather dull, more or less elliptical leaves, with fairly large flowers of intense purple which might claim relationship to 'Blue Boy; and the Commodore group with glossy quilted leaves and blue-purple flowers, such as 'Admiral' and 'Neptune'. These groups, however, are not well defined and one is hard put at times to decide just where a variety belongs. There are, however, some with definite characteristics as defined below.

Amazon and Supreme These are varieties which originated as mutations, reputedly, from leaf cuttings of the varieties whose names form part of their own cognomen—'Amazon Pink' (mutation of 'Pink Beauty'), 'Blue Boy Supreme', et cetera. There is no real distinction between Amazons and Supremes. Plants which inspired the distinguishing appellations apparently originated in two different establishments at about the same time. One of the originators called the break Amazon and the other hit on the name Supreme. The African Violet Society decided which of these names should be used before or after the remaining part of the name—'Blue Boy Supreme', 'Amazon Pink' are the officially registered forms in the Master Variety List.

The Amazons and Supremes, in general, are varieties with heavier, usually rounded foliage and larger flowers than the variety from which they originated. For example, in 'Blue Girl Supreme' the flowers are averaging about a quarter inch larger

'Double Blue Boy' is also known as 'Double Duchess', 'Duchess', or 'Double Russian', and is probably the first double-flowered variety to be introduced. This is now a collector's item.

than those of 'Blue Girl', and the leafstalks are thicker. My notes on this variety include such phrases as: "Flowers well displayed; clean cut, with white, green-tinged throat. They look big; rich and velvety." I have grown a number of Supremes and Amazons, but mostly they leave me cold, chiefly because they are slow-growing and seem less able to adapt themselves to the slings and arrows of outrageous cultural conditions. Even though the individual flowers are often magnificent, they are not produced so freely as those of their prototypes, consequently their decorative value on the whole is less. 'Athena', a double white flower edged in blue, and 'White Pride Supreme', a double white flower, are currently popular hybrids with Amazon-Supreme foliage and growth habit.

Double-flowered Varieties The one thing these have in common is their multiplicity of petals. To me one of the great charms of *Saintpaulia* is the form of the flower and its contrasting stamens. I see no beauty in the shape of the doubles which seem to consist of a mass of numerous, misshapen petals. However, some modern double varieties have the beauty of form approaching that of Camellias and Roses. The flowers of the double saintpaulias do have the merit of long-lastingness, but, on the other hand, the plants are sometimes shy bloomers, and the flower stalks often fail to elongate enough to display the flowers.

(*Editor's Note: These characteristics are largely overcome in some of the modern semidouble Rhapsodie and Ballet hybrids and in the popular new types such as 'Miriam Steel' and 'Candy Lips Improved'. C.M.F.*)

Du Pont Varieties These were originated by Mrs. William K. Du Pont from seed by a program of crossing and rigorous selection. They possess some of the characteristics of the Amazons and Supremes and are capable of developing into enormous plants. The leaves are massive and meaty with almost orbicular blades, stiff and unyielding as cardboard, up to 6 inches across.

'Du Pont Lavender Pink' has very large, pale red-violet flowers which often measure three inches across. A plant may reach massive proportions. This is now a collector's item.

In many of the varieties, the papillae are more conspicuous than usual. The stalks are of pencil thickness, or even more, and are exceedingly brittle; and, in general, they radiate almost horizontally from the center, making a flattish rosette. These characteristics exasperate the commercial growers, who experience great difficulty in packing them for safe shipment. The flowers, in a good range of colors, may be up to 3 inches across and, considering their size, are produced rather freely. Often a plant will throw a few aberrant flowers, some with four petals and double the normal number of stamens, or they may be radially, instead of bilaterally, symmetrical. I like the Du Ponts for their distinctiveness and massiveness. They grow too large for cramped quarters and seem to be among the first to catch anything available in the form of pests and diseases—thrips, mites, nematodes, and crown rots. But they are magnificent when well grown.

Girl and My Lady Varieties 'Blue Girl,' the first of the Girls, originated as a sport of 'Blue Boy', which it resembles except for the leaves characteristic of the series, which are rounded, deeply scalloped when young, with pale markings radiating into the veins at the junction of stalk and blade. Sometimes the pale area is reduced to a tiny streak. Sometimes it occupies almost half the area of the blade with markings along the edge, especially at the base of the sinuses. When the leafstalk is reddish, often the coloring may extend into the pale area, giving a tricolored effect. The scallops may extend into definite lobes. In 'Blue Girl Compacta', the basal lobes may develop spirally to give the effect of a snail's shell; and in 'Old Lace', the crenations and lobes are puckered like blisters. In the Girl and My Lady varieties (essentially the same), the chief defect in my experience is the occasional failure of the leafstalks to elongate, so that the center becomes congested and the flower stalks contorted and twisted in their endeavors to reach the light. (This may also be a manifestation of mite injury.) Many of these varieties are less constant in bloom than the usual run of saintpaulias; but, nevertheless, they are worth growing for the beauty of their foliage alone. 'Pink A Poppin', a semidouble pink, is a popular hybrid with Girl foliage.

Trailers New trailing African-violets are delightful subjects for hanging baskets, tray gardens, and terrarium plantings. The miniature trailers are especially charming in large dish gardens and terrarium landscapes. All of the trailers look lovely in light gardens, trained along shelves to hide pots of other plants.

Many of the new trailing hybrids have been developed by hybridizer Lyndon Lyon and his popular selections are listed in several national mail-order catalogues. The trailing types grow multiple crowns on gradually spreading stems. If plants become ragged-looking, just cut back the longer stems, root the stem tips for more plants, and wait for the older clump to leaf out again.

Older stems that are cut back soon sprout new crowns, so pruning is the best way to keep trailers bushy and floriferous. Some modern trailers well worth growing are:

> *'Coral Trail'*, a double-flowered coral-pink.
> *'Freedom Trail'*, a double-flowered fuchsia-colored hybrid.
> *'Gypsy Trail'*, a double-flowered light pink, vigorous trailer.
> *'Happy Trails'*, a semiminiature with double dark pink flowers.
> *'Jet Trails'*, a double-flowered wisteria blue semiminiature.
> *'Lora Lou,'* double pink flowers on semiminiature plant with variegated foliage.
> *'Mysterium'*, a double-flowered pink trailer, medium green foliage.
> *'Pixie Blue'*, an outstanding miniature with small leaves, blue single flowers, compact trailing habit.

Spoon-leaved Varieties The spooning character in which the edges of the leaves turn upward and expose part of the lower surface does not seem to be any too constant. One could theorize that this is an inherited tendency in which the immediate stimulus is a cessation of growth followed by recrudescence in which the cells in the vicinity of the edges do not take part and thus the latter must perforce turn either up or down—in this case up. 'Neptune' and miniature 'Pink Trinket' are varieties in which this character is likely to appear. Variations on spooning are heavily fluted leaves with partially turned-up edges, called holly-type foliage.

The novice is likely to be confused by the multiplicity of names and wonders where to begin. So, here, in alphabetical order, are some classic varieties selected on the basis of beauty, ease of culture, and distinctiveness from each other.

CLASSIC SELECTIONS

These seven older varieties, originally described by Mr. Free, are still available from some saintpaulia specialists.

'Admiral' makes a handsome, symmetrical plant, with shining quilted leaves and medium-size flowers of red-violet to deep violet. It blooms very freely and is one of the best for summer display.

'Amethyst' is an old favorite, very free-flowering, with pale lavender blooms (the two upper petals slightly darker) about 1½ inches across. The leaves on long petioles are broadly heart-shaped, toothed, and glossy; sometimes reddish beneath. Not so strong a grower as the darker-hued 'Admiral' which I personally prefer in this type.

'Blue Boy' is still, in my experience, the best all-round variety. It is easily grown, blooms profusely over a long period with deep blue-violet flowers usually 1½ inches across but which occasionally approach a diameter of 2 inches. However, at least one

'Amethyst' is almost constantly crowded with lavender flowers.

*'Blue Boy' is one of the most good-natured of all African-violet
varieties and a classic, with deep blue-violet flowers.*

commercial grower has given it up because it "lacks vigor" due,
in his opinion, to overpropagation—a belief which probably
cannot be substantiated.

'Commodore'   A strong grower: a plant in a 3½-inch pot is capable of exceeding 16 inches across. The leaves are glossy,
quilted, and flushed with rose beneath. The flowers, about 1¾
inches across, are rich purple with the petals fringed, more con-
spicuously than usual, with tiny white hairs.

'Neptune'   has fairly deep violet flowers with faint darker stria-
tions. They are freely produced and carried well above the foliage; the petals overlap and the general effect is of a rounded
flower. The leaves are handsome, lustrous, deep green, rosy-pur-
ple beneath, broad-oval with rounded tips. They are heavily

'Viking' is a prolific bloomer. The deep blue-violet flowers are often so liberally produced as to hide the foliage.

quilted; sometimes puckered into "blisters." Some specimens are heavily spooned, but this character is not constant. Spooned or not, it is a first-class variety.

'Norseman' The flowers of this well-known variety are blue-violet (almost a "true" medium blue) clustered just above the rosette. The number of petals on some flowers may be four; in some cases six to eight. The leaves are dull to lustrous, oval, quilted, flushed with rose-purple beneath.

'Viking' sometimes blooms so freely as almost to obscure foliage. The flowers are small (about 1 inch), deep blue-violet and, like those of 'Ruffles', may have a variable number of petals, more than the usual number of stamens, and once in a while a pure-white petal or two. Sometimes sets seed without artificial pollination. The leaves are purplish-red beneath, heavily quilted, slightly glossy.

MODERN HYBRID STRAINS

Growers who specialize in saintpaulias as show plants do not mind fussing over novelty hybrids if the final flowers are spectacular enough. However, most people grow house plants as decoration and just for fun, rather than to win prizes at a show or beat their neighbors in having something unique.

For this reason, special success has come to the breeders who have specialized in creating adapable, easily grown saintpaulias. Two modern strains are now world-famous for their ability to be almost constantly in bloom under varied conditions. The Rhapsodie saintpaulia hybrids, developed by Hermann Holtkamp in Isselburg, West Germany, and the Ballet hybrids created by Arnold Fischer, formerly of Hannover, Germany, have convinced thousands of gardeners that African-violets are not hard to grow.

By developing hybrids that are vigorous and uniform, the hybridizers Holtkamp and Fischer have been able to patent their creations and arrange for mass marketing. The Rhapsodie and Ballet strain hybrids are found in garden centers, supermarkets, florists, and specialty boutiques everywhere. Growers have

'Rhapsodie Elfriede', a widely grown dark blue hybrid, is typical of the newer African-violets which largely replace the old classics such as deep violet-blue 'Viking', one of the original Armacost and Royston series.

learned that with modest basic care these delightful modern strains are sure to provide years of pleasure.

Since Ballet and Rhapsodie hybrids are patented, they cost slightly more than non-patented plants, to cover a modest royalty required for each plant sold. However, the slight extra cost is more than offset by the assurance that these fully tested African-violets have the highest chance to grow well for you.

Reinholdt Holtkamp, son of the Rhapsodie strain originator Hermann Holtkamp, has recently developed a new series of modern hybrids called the Optimara strain. The individual clones are named after the fifty United States of America. The Optimaras are noted for quick growth and very full bunches of flowers well held above the foliage.

The Geo. J. Ball Co., United States distributor of the Ballet hybrids, has a continuing program of development to test and introduce new hybrids created by Arnold Fischer, who now resides in California.

If you are just starting with African-violets, it would be wise to begin your collection with several plants selected from these sturdy strains. Since they are bred for vigor, they will tolerate slightly less than perfect culture and are thus excellent types with which to learn African-violet growing.

UNUSUAL HYBRIDS

Very unusual hybrids, including those with variegated foliage, odd leaf patterns, unique floral shapes or color breaks due to mutations, and other attractive variations, are not stable enough for mass propagation or marketing. For this reason, the firms which propagate African-violets for shipment by the thousands to wholesale outlets cannot afford to sell such variations. If a hybrid is advertised as having variegated foliage or specific color break in the blooms, but then does not propagate 100 per cent true, from leaves, the mass distributor has problems with advertising, plant patent protection, and consumer acceptance.

Therefore, to obtain the most unusual and the very newest African-violets, you must order from one of the specialty breeders. For example, Lyndon Lyon has developed many different miniatures, trailers, variegated hybrids, and selections with different color combinations. Other breeders have introduced hybrids with fringed flowers, green-edged blooms, star-shaped flowers, and other unusual forms. These plants are not under patent nor are they distributed in supermarkets or big garden stores. However, you can obtain these new creations directly from the breeders and from specialist growers who advertise in the Society publications. Some of the larger mail-order firms and African-violet specialty nurseries are listed in Chapter 13.

The early African-violets mentioned by name throughout this book are still grown by a few commercial places and home growers. National shows often have an honored section reserved for the classic varieties, including the original Armacost and Royston hybrids that did so much to popularize African-violets in America.

For the non-specialist grower and the beginner, modern hybrids bred for extra vigor, adaptability, and continuous flowering are recommended. The twelve standard-size hybrids described here are excellent plants that are sure to thrive under average house plant growing conditions. These have also been selected on the basis of floral beauty and uniqueness.

'*Ballet Abby*', flat white flowers, round green leaves.

'*Ballet Dolly*', frilled white flowers with blue edge.

'*Ballet Lisa*', large single glowing pink, dark green leaves.

'*Ballet Ulli*', clusters of frilled dark blue flowers, neat growth.

'*Jennifer*', unique single flowers in light lavender with dark plum border, whole flower edged in silver hairs.

'*Miriam Steel*', double-fringed white flowers sometimes tinged with pink, very popular.

'*New York*', a very dark velvety blue Optimara strain hybrid.

'*Nevada*', unusual Optimara with frilled white flowers edged in purple.

'*Rhapsodie Elfriede*', rich dark blue with yellow anthers.

'*Rhapsodie Ophelia*', a plum-red semidouble with darker center, dark green foliage blushed maroon.

'*Tipt*', unusual single lavender flowers with dark lavender tip on each petal.

'*Tommie Lou*', popular white-flowered clone, flowers often marked pink in center, plain quilted dark green foliage variegated along edge with white.

VARIEGATED HYBRIDS

African-violets are famous for their frequent mutations—such as changes in leaf pattern, flower color, and petal form. Among the most attractive variations are variegated leaves. Some variegated

Miniature African-violets come with variegated leaves, such as this seedling from Lyndon Lyon's hybridizing program.

hybrids have liberal amounts of cream or green-gold coloration, especially in the center of each plant—most noticeably in the younger leaves. Other types have a thin edge of white, sometimes blushed pink, on the margin of each leaf. Still others have liberal splashings of gold or white throughout the foliage.

These foliage variations are not too stable. Cultural conditions often cause the variegation to alter its pattern, almost disappear, or become more intense. For these reasons, variegated hybrids are seldom seen in mass market outlets, but are available from specialist growers. Now there are even miniature variegated hybrids and variegated foliage on trailing plants. Some of the most attractive recent introductions are listed here.

> '*Cordelia*', a double-flowered pink with variable white edges on the foliage.
> '*Happy Harold*', a single burgundy-red flower over variegated leaves resembling those on 'Tommie Lou'.
> '*Lilian Jarrett*', a peach-pink informal double flower with gold and cream splashed leaves.
> '*Little Lou*', a miniature with double dark blue flowers, white-edged leaves sometimes blushed pink.
> '*Lora Lou*', a semiminiature trailer with double lavender-pink flowers, variable pattern of white on foliage.
> '*Midget Bon Bon*', a miniature with single pink flowers, cream and gold variegated leaves.
> '*Mr. Gus*', a double purple flower, gold-toned foliage.
> '*Nancy Reagan*', double wine-red flowers, foliage blotched white.
> '*Tommie Lou*', double white flowers often tinged pink, variable pattern of white on foliage edges.

Culture   Grow variegated plants on the cool side, 60° to 70°, and under bright conditions for the best variegation. Fertilize with a low-nitrogen formula such as Peters Variegated Violet Special 5-50-17.

THE BEST VARIETIES LIST

Each year the African Violet Society of America compiles a list of favorite African-violets, based on votes cast by the Society members. Each year the list changes, as new plants become better known, show plants become popular, old favorites prove themselves excellent choices for home growing. The hybrids receiving the most votes are listed first, while those gaining fewer votes are listed last.

The top twenty-five varieties listed for 1977 are an interesting cross section of internationally distributed mass-produced cultivars and special show-type selections often grown by specialists. Here are the top twenty-five for 1977, each followed by the hybridizer who created the plant.

> *'Miriam Steel'*, double white, Granger.
> *'Tommie Lou'*, double white and orchid, white feathered foliage, Oden.
> *'Garnet Elf'*, rose-lavender single with white border, Granger.
> *'Tina'*, double garnet-fuchsia, Maas.
> *'Nancy Reagan'*, double wine-red, variegated foliage, Rienhardt.
> *'Rhapsodie Mars'*, ruby red single, Holtkamp.
> *'Happy Harold'*, wine-red single, variegated foliage, Rienhardt.
> *'Lullaby'*, light blue double, white shading, Granger.
> *'Ballet Lisa'*, frilled single pink, Fischer.
> *'Firebird'*, fringed single, red center, white border, Granger.
> *'Triple Threat'*, double pink star, Lyon.
> *'Granger's Serenity'*, double white, dark purple edge, Granger.
> *'Rhapsodie Gigi'*, semidouble white, blue border, Holtkamp.
> *'Lilian Jarrett'*, pink double, variegated foliage, Tinari.
> *'Delft Imperial'*, double two-tone blue flowers, Granger.

'*Top Dollar*', double blue-purple flower, variegated foliage, Rienhardt.

'*Ballet Marta*', single lavender, frilled petals, Fischer.

'*Granger's Fashionaire*', double lavender pink, Granger.

'*Mary D*', double red star, Maas.

'*Rhapsodie Elfriede*', single dark blue, Holtkamp.

'*Starshine*', single white star, Granger.

'*Granger's Peach Frost*', double ivory peach, copper-tipped, Granger.

'*Helene*', semidouble fuchsia red, Lyon.

'*Spring Deb*', double white with ruffled blue edge, Granger.

'*Butterfly White*', semidouble white star, Lyon.

Outstanding hybrids may not be on the list because they are not yet well enough known or distributed to AVSA members to receive votes. However, those hybrids that do appear on the list, as the most popular twenty-five selections, are good choices for showy plants, well worth adding to your collection.

Plants that appear on the Best Varieties List for five consecutive years are listed on the Honor Roll of African Violets, published in the *African Violet Magazine*. Honor Roll hybrids are naturally older selections than those found as the top twenty-five selections of a current Best Varieties List, but the Honor Roll plants have passed a tough test of providing satisfactory performance for at least five years in a row. With so many hybrids being introduced each year, the AVSA Best Varieties List and Honor Roll provide a guide for selecting proven hybrids.

BEST MINIATURES

The African Violet Society does not yet publish a list of favorite miniatures and semiminiatures but Mrs. Sidney Bogin, chairman of the Mini and Semimini Classification Committee of the AVSA, reports that such a project is under consideration. Mrs. Bogin reported, in 1977, that the plants continuously seen as show winners and as favorites with specialists in miniatures are those listed below.

'*Blue Sprite*', double light blue, Lyon.
'*Dancing Doll*', double pink, Lyon.
'*Little Jim*', double pink, Maas.
'*Tiny Gypsy*', single fuchsia, Lyon.
'*Denim Blue*', double blue, Lyon.
Midget Bon Bon', single pink, Champion.
'*Midget Midnight*', single royal blue, Champion.
'*Midget Valentine*', fuchsia red, Champion.
'*Icicle Trinket*', double white, variegated foliage, Champion.
'*Candy Trinket*', double pink and white, variegated, Champion.
'*Royal Trinket*', double royal blue, variegated foliage, Champion.
'*Little Red*', single red, Maas.
'*Little Rascal*', semidouble blue-splashed pink, Lyon.
'*Wee Lass*', double white, red edge, Lyon.
'*Double Take*', double pansy purple, Lyon.
'*Tiny Teen*', double red-pink, often part white, Lyon.
'*Tiny Sparkles*', double burgundy mauve, white dots, Lyon.
'*Cradle Song*', semidouble heliotrope star, E. Fisher.
'*Little Delight*', double white, frilled purple edge, Lyon.
'*Sweet Pixie*', double light pink, Swift.
'*Dora Baker*', double pink, Lorenzen.
'*Mini-Mignon*', double amethyst star, Annalee.

To Mrs. Bogin's excellent and helpful list I would add two of my favorite miniatures, based on their outstanding growth and continuous display of dainty blooms in my light garden:

'*High Stepper*', single pink, very compact, Lyon.
'*Pixie Blue*', single blue trailer, Lyon.

The AVSA does publish a complete variety list of miniature and semiminiature hybrids. This booklet can be obtained for $2.00

from Mrs. Sidney Bogin, 39 Boyd St., Long Beach, N.Y. 11561. For those who wish to collect only small-growing African-violets, this booklet is very helpful. Additional information on the miniatures is found in the *African Violet Magazine* under Ellie Bogin's "Musings from the Mini-Mam" heading.

CONCLUSION

In our present stage of knowledge it is impossible to describe, classify, and evaluate *all* the varieties of saintpaulia. They are changelings, sensitive to environment, and doubtless soil and climate difference influence their behavior. The stage of growth at which they are seen cannot fail to color the reactions of the observer in his estimate of their value.

I have grown in our home as many picked varieties (more than seventy) culled from nine different sources as the house could accommodate. I have been in close touch with Ed. Wentink of the Rose Acre Nurseries, Salisbury Mills, New York, a nearby grower who tries to include all the best in his collection of more than one hundred varieties, the content of which is constantly changing. In addition, I have visited the greenhouses of a dozen or more other dealers to observe saintpaulias. I have looked over the varieties displayed at the conventions of the African Violet Society and in many private homes. But I am frank to admit that there must be some good varieties that have not received mention here; and there are many which have not been available for a period long enough to prove their worth, and many which will be introduced after these lines are written.

New varieties are being put on the market at an alarming rate; and when the offsprings of the crosses between the newly introduced species and existing varieties begin to appear, confusion will be worse confounded unless the growers co-operate fully with the Registration Committee of the African Violet Society, develop a strong sense of responsibility in respect to making new names, and do all they can to eliminate unworthy varieties and duplicates. As knowledge grows, I believe we shall find that some varieties are more resistant to disease, mites and insects, and should be pushed to the exclusion of those which are susceptible; we shall find that the light and water requirements of varieties vary and this should be noted in the catalogues of dealers to guide the purchaser in acquiring those best adapted to his conditions.

The possibilities for developing new forms of *Saintpaulia,* which are improvements on existing varieties, good though they are, are almost unlimited, and it will be many years before the last word can be said regarding them and their culture.

RECENT ADVANCES

Since the original edition of *All About African Violets,* several major advances have occurred in the techniques of commercial hybridizing, growing, and marketing. International hybridizers such as the Holtkamp firm in Germany, developers of the Optimara strain, and Arnold Fischer, developer of the Ballet strain, make thousands of hybrids each year. Millions of seedlings are grown and only a few very choice individuals are selected for introduction. Such mass marketing requires that new hybrids propagate quickly, with several plantlets forming from each leaf. The mass-marketed African-violets must also make a big show of long-lasting flowers quickly and then maintain the flowering habit all year long.

Foliage must be uniform and attractive, plants must adapt to different conditions. All of the commercial requirements have produced a group of modern hybrids that are easy to grow, very showy, and widely distributed. African-violets are now a plant for every home, not just the specialist. Experiments have already been done on producing select hybrids by tissue culture, a technique widely used for orchids. So far, growing African-violets from tissue is more expensive than growing them from leaves, but soon techniques may be refined and costs lowered. Tissue culture permits a grower to obtain thousands of identical plants from a single growing point (meristem); thus a new hybrid could be mass-produced and offered to the public in a year rather than the several years now required.

CHAPTER 13

Sources of Plants and Supplies

Plants and growing supplies can sometimes be found at stores just around the corner from your home, but often the newest hybrids can only be purchased from growers who may be several states or a country away. So it may also be with some growing supplies, including unusual pots and unique fertilizers. Fortunately plants and supplies can easily be ordered by mail.

PLANTS BY MAIL

The African-violet shipping season is from April until about mid-November over most of the country. During colder months it is dangerous to have these cold-tender gesneriads sent through the mails, even with careful packing. During the regular shipping season, from spring into mid-fall, you will have no trouble receiving excellent African-violets and fresh-cut leaves from numerous mail-order nurseries. Ordering plants by mail is sometimes the only way to get the classic older hybrids or the very latest novelty, unless you happen to live within driving distance of a commercial grower who has what you want.

Buy your plants from firms which specialize in supplying healthy, well-grown African-violets or fresh-cut ready-to-root leaves. However, something can always go wrong when we are dealing with living plants, so never hesitate to inform the seller if you receive a plant with free mealybugs or a shipment that is badly damaged.

PERSONAL SELECTION

If you live near a nursery or can visit a commercial saintpaulia specialist at any time, by all means arrange to see plants in person. Many nurseries welcome visitors during regular working hours while others request that you call for an appointment. The companies listed below are among the many reputable suppliers of saintpaulias around the country which should be able to satisfy your needs. The plant society magazines are another source to locate saintpaulia growers near you.

COMPANY	OFFERINGS
Annalee Violetry 29–50 214th Place Bayside, NY 11360	Free listing of show types, including new miniatures and trailers. Send business-size stamped envelope.
Buell's Greenhouses Eastford, CT 06242	Free list for large stamped envelope. Many gesneriads.
W. Atlee Burpee Co. Warminster, PA 18974	Free color illustrated catalogue includes African-violets and growing supplies.
Fischer Greenhouses Linwood, NJ 08221	Plant catalogue for 15¢ includes many African-violets. Growing supply catalogue, 25¢.
Floralite Co. 4124 East Oakwood Road Oak Creek, WI 53154	Free lists of indoor light gardening supplies, plant stands, sprayers.

The Green House
9515 Flower St.
Bellflower, CA 90706

Free brochure of Gro-Cart light gardening stand. Plants for sale at the nursery only.

Bernard D. Greeson
3548 North Cramer
Milwaukee, WI 53211

Catalogue of growing supplies, including potting materials, 35¢.

Heavenly Violets
Mrs. Mary V. Boose
9 Turney Place
Trumbill, CT 06611

List for 25¢ includes the original 10 Armacost and Royston hybrids, plus many new hybrids.

Indoor Gardening Supplies
P.O. Box 40567
Detroit, MI 48240

Free illustrated catalogue of supplies with many items for light gardening.

Albert G. Krieger
1063 Cranbrook Drive
Jackson, MI 49201

List for 25¢ includes the 10 original Armacost and Royston hybrids, plus many modern hybrids.

Lord and Burnham Co.
Irvington, NY 10533

Free catalogue of greenhouses and some growing supplies.

Lyndon Lyon
Dolgeville, NY 13329

Free catalogue for first-class stamp. Original hybrids.

Marko Co.
94 Porete Ave.
North Arlington, NJ 07032

Free illustrated list of light garden fixtures with wedged louvers to hide the lamps.

Mellinger's
2310 West South Range Road
North Lima, OH 44452

Free comprehensive catalogue of growing supplies, potting mixes, some plants.

Geo. W. Park Seed Co.
P.O. Box 31
Greenwood, SC 29647

Free catalogue contains African-violets and growing supplies.

Robert B. Peters Co.
2833 Pennsylvania St.
Allentown, PA 18104

Free catalogue of chemical water-soluble fertilizers.

St. Louis Violet Nurseries
2662 Smoke View Drive
Maryland Heights, MO 63043

Specialist in hybrid seed and leaves of new hybrids. Free list for stamped self-addressed envelope or 25¢ in coin.

Shoplite Co.
566 Franklin Ave.
Nutley, NJ 07110

Complete catalogue of light garden supplies and plant stands, 25¢.

Texas Greenhouse Co.
2717 St. Louis Ave.
Fort Worth, TX 76110

Free illustrated catalogue of growing supplies and greenhouses.

Tinari Greenhouses
2325 Valley Road
Huntingdon Valley, PA 19006

Color illustrated catalogue for 25¢, includes many unusual hybrids, growing supplies, light fixtures.

Tube Craft Inc.
1311 West 80th St.
Cleveland, OH 44102

Free folder shows Flora Carts and related light garden supplies.

Glossary

EXPLANATION OF TECHNICAL TERMS

ABERRANT   Varying from what is usual.

ACUTE   Applied to a leaf or petal with pointed tip.

ANTHER   Pollen-bearing part of the stamen.

AXIL   Upper angle made by petiole where it joins the stem.

BI-GENERIC HYBRID   The result of a cross between two genera.

BLADE   The expanded part of a leaf.

BULLATE   Having a puckered or blistered-looking surface.

CALYX   A collective term for sepals; the outer circle of the floral envelope.

CAPSULE   A dry fruit with more than one compartment.

CHROMOSOMES   Tiny bodies found within the cell nucleus, which contain the genes.

COMPOUND LEAF   One with two or more separate leaflets.

CORDATE   A leaf with a sinus and two rounded lobes at the base of the blade; heart-shaped.

COROLLA   The petals, or lobes, collectively of a flower.

COTYLEDONS   Seed leaves; in *Saintpaulia* (and many other plants) they emerge from the seed coat and are the first leaves to become visible.

CRENATE   With shallow round teeth.

CROWN   In saintpaulia parlance it is a single rosette of leaves or a growing point capable of growing into a rosette.

CULTIVAR   An individual clone or variety found mainly in horticulture and propagated vegetatively.

CYME   A broad flower cluster with the main stalk terminated by a flower which opens in advance of the rest.

DENTATE   Toothed with the teeth spreading outward.

DOUBLE   Flowers with more than usual number of petals.

ELLIPTIC   A narrow, curved outline with rounded ends.

ENTIRE   Margin not indented.

FILAMENT   Stalk of the anther.

FLUTED   Leaves channeled or grooved.

GAMOPETALOUS   A corolla having the petals wholly or partially united.

GENERA   Plural of genus.

GENUS   A group of species linked by botanical characters, and more like each other than those of any other group.

HEART-SHAPED   Oval in general outline but with two rounded basal lobes; cordate.

LIP   The lowermost lobe of the *Saintpaulia* corolla is sometimes called the "lip."

LOBE   A part of corolla or leaf divided to about the middle.

MIDRIB   The principal vein of a leaf.

MULTIPLE CROWN   Name given to describe a *Saintpaulia* plant with more than one rosette of leaves.

MUTATION   A hereditary change in character not due to crossing. A mutation, or "sport," may originate from a seedling or vegetatively as a "bud mutation" when a branch becomes altered to produce a different type of flower or fruit; or when the plantlets originating from a *Saintpaulia* leaf cutting differ from their parent.

OBTUSE   Leaf with a rounded apex.

OFFSET   A plant arising close to base of mother plant; also applied to side shoots or crowns originating from main stem of *Saintpaulia*.

OVARY   The part of a pistil which bears the ovules which, when fertilized, develop into seeds.

OVATE   Shaped like the silhouette of a hen's egg with the broad part nearest to the petiole.

PEDICEL   The stalk of a single flower in a cluster.

PEDUNCLE   The stalk of a solitary flower or the main stalk of a cluster.

PETAL   One of the separate parts of a corolla. Although the divisions of a *Saintpaulia* corolla are popularly called petals it would be more correct to speak of them as corolla lobes because they are united at the base (gamopetalous).

PETIOLE   The stalk of a leaf.

PINKED   Crenate or scalloped.

PISTIL   The seed-bearing organ consisting of ovary, style, and stigma.

POLLEN   Small particles, often granular or powdery, containing male elements, borne by the anthers.

POLLINATION   The act of transferring pollen from an anther to a stigma.

POSTICOUS   Situated on the outer side.

SCALLOPED   Having an undulating edge; in saintpaulia parlance a form of crenation in which the projections are exaggerated.

SEPAL   One of the separate parts of a calyx.

SINUS   Any recess between two lobes—of leaf or corolla.

SLICK   Presumably, sleek; smooth and shining appearance.

SPECIES   A species is a group of individuals alike in all characteristics and belonging to a single genus.

SPOONED   Leaves with the margin prominently turned upward.

STALK   The stem of a flower, anther, leaf, et cetera.

STERILE   Has several applications: a rooting medium lacking in nutrients; soil that has been treated with heat or chemicals to destroy disease organisms; certain hybrids which are unable to produce seeds, et cetera.

STIGMA   The area, usually at the top of a pistil, which receives the pollen.

STYLE   The part of the pistil between ovary and stigma.

SUBACUTE   Nearly acute.

TAILORED   I haven't been able to figure this one, sometimes applied to flowers and foliage. Neat?

UMBEL   A cluster of flowers with stems of about equal length arising from a common center.

VEINS   The skeleton of the leaf which strengthens the blade and serves as conducting tissue.

VENATION   Arrangement of veins in the leaf—parallel, feathered, netted.

PRONUNCIATION OF SCIENTIFIC NAMES USED IN THIS BOOK (Based on *The Home Garden Self-Pronouncing Dictionary of Plant Names*)

Genera and Plant Families

Achimenes—Ak-*kim*-en-eez

Columnea—Kol-*lum*-nee-uh

Conandron—Kon-*and*-ron

Corytholoma (Gesneria)—Koh-rith-oh-*loh*-muh

Episcia—Ep-*piss*-see-uh

Gesneria—Jez-*neer*-ee-uh

Gesneriaceae—Jez-neer-ee-*ay*-see-e

Haberlea—Hay-*ber*-lee-uh

Kohleria—Ko-*leer*-ee-uh

Petrocosmea—Pet-roh-*kos*-me-uh

Ramonda—Ray-*mond*-uh

Saintpaulia—Saint-*paul*-ee-uh

Sinningia—Sin-*nin*-jee-uh

Smithiantha (Gesneria, Naegelia—Nee-*jeel*-ee-uh)—Smith-ee-*anth*-uh

Streptocarpus—Strep-toh-*karp*-us

Umbelliferae—Um-bel-*lif*-fer-ee

Viola—*Vye*-ol-uh

Violaceae—Vye-o-*lay*-see-ee

Species

amaniensis—am-an-ee-*en*-siss; of Amani
diplotricha—dip-loh-*trik*-uh; hairs of two kinds
goetzeana—get-zee-*ay*-nuh; commemorative name
grotei—*groh*-tee-eye; commemorative name
ionantha—eye-oh-*nanth*-uh; flowers like a Violet
kewensis—kew-*en*-siss; of Kew
magungensis—may-gun-*jen-siss;* of Magunga
orbicularis—or-bik-yew-*lay*-riss; round
priceana—prye-see-*ay*-nuh; commemorative name
pusilla—pew-*sill*-uh; small
tongwensis—ton-*gwen*-siss; of Tongwe

Index